HMH Georgia Science

This Write-In Book belongs to

_____

Teacher/Room

_____

Houghton Mifflin Harcourt™

Consulting Authors

Michael A. DiSpezio
Global Educator
North Falmouth, Massachusetts

Marjorie Frank
Science Writer and Content-Area Reading
  Specialist
Brooklyn, New York

Michael Heithaus
Dean, College of Arts and Sciences
Florida International University
North Miami, Florida

Georgia Reviewers

C. Alex Alvarez, Ed.D
Director of STEM and Curriculum
Valdosta City Schools
Valdosta, Georgia

Kristen N. Brooks
2nd Grade Teacher
Lindsey Elementary School
Warner Robins, Georgia

Melissa Davis
K–5 Science Coordinator
Atlanta Public Schools
Atlanta, Georgia

Natasha Luster-Knighton
5th Grade Science Teacher
Radium Springs Elementary
Albany, Georgia

Amy Materne
Russell Elementary School
Warner Robins, Georgia

Erin Neal
2nd Grade Teacher
White Oak Elementary School
Newnan, Georgia

Mark Christian Rheault
K–5 Specialist
Union County Elementary
Blairsville, Georgia

Kolenda Thomas-McDavis
5th Grade Science Ambassador
Northside Elementary
Warner Robins, Georgia

Christina Voigt
Teacher
Lake Joy Elementary
Warner Robins, Georgia

Dora A. Waite
Georgia State Science Ambassador
Russell Elementary
Warner Robins, Georgia

Contents

Levels of Inquiry Key ■ DIRECTED ■ GUIDED ■ INDEPENDENT

THE NATURE OF SCIENCE AND S.T.E.M.

Unit 1—How Scientists Work 1

Lesson 1 What Are Senses and Other Tools? 3
Inquiry Flipchart p. 2—Shoebox Senses/Balancing Act

Inquiry Lesson 2 How Can We Use Our Senses? 15
Inquiry Flipchart p. 3—How Can We Use Our Senses?

Lesson 3 What Are Inquiry Skills? 17
Inquiry Flipchart p. 4—Measure Up/Animal Models

Inquiry Lesson 4 How Do We Use Inquiry Skills? 27
Inquiry Flipchart p. 5—How Do We Use Inquiry Skills?

Lesson 5 How Do Scientists Work? 29
Inquiry Flipchart p. 6—Holding Water/My Fingerprints

People in Science: Mary Anderson 39

Unit 1 Review 41

✓ # Unit 2—Technology All Around Us.......... 45

Lesson 1 How Do Engineers Work? 47
Inquiry Flipchart p. 7—Don't Crack Up!/Make It Fly!

Inquiry Lesson 2 How Can We Solve a Problem? 59
Inquiry Flipchart p. 8—How Can We Solve a Problem?

Lesson 3 What Materials Make Up Objects? 61
Inquiry Flipchart p. 9—Build It!/Materials Mission

Inquiry Lesson 4 How Can Materials Be Sorted? 73
Inquiry Flipchart p. 10—How Can Materials Be Sorted?

People in Science: Dr. Eugene Tssui 75

Unit 2 Review 77

EARTH SCIENCE

Unit 3—Weather and Seasons 81

Lesson 1 What Is Weather?.................................... 83
Inquiry Flipchart p. 11—Hot or Cold?/Make a Pinwheel

S1E1.b

Inquiry Lesson 2 What Can We Observe About Weather?....... 97
Inquiry Flipchart p. 12—What Can We Observe About Weather?

S1E1.a, S1E1.c

People in Science: June Bacon-Bercey 101

Lesson 3 What Are Seasons? 103
Inquiry Flipchart p. 13—Keeping Warm/Turn Over a New Leaf

S1E1.d

S.T.E.M. Engineering and Technology: Weather Wisdom............ 115
Inquiry Flipchart p. 14—Build It: Rain Gauge

S1E1.c

Unit 3 Review 117

PHYSICAL SCIENCE

Unit 4—Light and Sound 121

Lesson 1 What Is Light?..................................... 123
Inquiry Flipchart p. 15—No Light, No Sight!/Light It Up

S1P1.a, S1P1.b

Inquiry Lesson 2 What Can We Learn About Shadows? 131
Inquiry Flipchart p. 16—What Can We Learn About Shadows?

S1P1.c

Lesson 3 What Is Sound?.................................... 133
Inquiry Flipchart p. 17—Water Music/Sound the Drum

S1P1.d

Inquiry Lesson 4 How Do We Make Sound? 143
Inquiry Flipchart p. 18—How Do We Make Sound?

S.T.E.M. Engineering and Technology: Call Me! Telephone Timeline... 145
Inquiry Flipchart p. 19— Design It: Make a Musical Instrument

S1P1.d

Lesson 5 How Can We Use Light and Sound? 147
Inquiry Flipchart p. 20—Light or Sound?/An Emergency Alert

S1P1.e

Careers in Science: Ask a Piano Tuner 155

Unit 4 Review 157

Unit 5—Magnets 161

Lesson 1 How Do Magnets Move Objects? 163
Inquiry Flipchart p. 21—Push and Pull/Which Magnet Will Win?

S1P2.a, S1P2.b

Inquiry Lesson 2 What Do Magnets Do? 173
Inquiry Flipchart p. 22—What Do Magnets Do?

S1P2.b

Careers in Science: Maglev Train Scientists 175

S1P2.a

S.T.E.M. Engineering and Technology: Magnets All Around 177
Inquiry Flipchart p. 23—Design It: Use Magnets

S1P2.a

Unit 5 Review 179

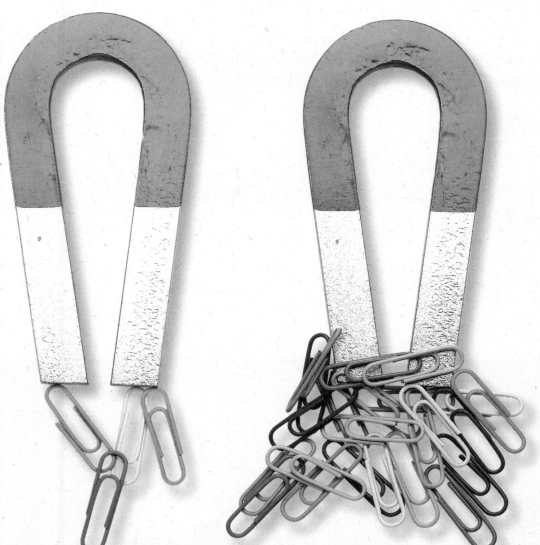

LIFE SCIENCE

Unit 6—Living Things

. . . . 183

Lesson 1 What Do Plants Need? 185
Inquiry Flipchart p. 24—Grow to the Light/**Colored Celery**

S1L1.b

Inquiry Lesson 2 Why Do Plants Grow? 195
Inquiry Flipchart p. 25—Why Do Plants Grow?

S1L1.b

Lesson 3 What Are Some Parts of Plants? 197
Inquiry Flipchart p. 26—Are All Seeds Alike?/**What Parts Do You See?**

S1L1.a

Lesson 4 What Do Animals Need? 207
Inquiry Flipchart p. 27—Meet the Mealworm/**Eat Like a Bird**

S1L1.b

Careers in Science: Ask a Zookeeper 219

S1L1.c

S.T.E.M. **Engineering and Technology:** Tool Time 221
Inquiry Flipchart p. 28—Design It: A New Tool

Unit 6 Review 223

21st Century Skills: Technology and Coding
. . . . 227

Interactive Glossary R1

Index R13

UNIT 1
How Scientists Work

Children's Museum,
Indianapolis, Indiana

Big Idea

Scientists use inquiry skills and tools to help them find out information.

I Wonder Why

Scientists study dinosaurs. Why?
Turn the page to find out.

Here's Why Scientists study dinosaurs to learn about animals that lived long ago.

In this unit, you will explore this Big Idea, the Essential Questions, and the Investigations on the Inquiry Flipchart.

Levels of Inquiry Key ■ DIRECTED ■ GUIDED ■ INDEPENDENT

Track Your Progress

Big Idea Scientists use inquiry skills and tools to help them find out information.

Essential Questions

Lesson 1 What Are Senses and Other Tools? 3
Inquiry Flipchart p. 2—Shoebox Senses/Balancing Act

Inquiry Lesson 2 How Can We Use Our Senses? 15
Inquiry Flipchart p. 3—How Can We Use Our Senses?

Lesson 3 What Are Inquiry Skills? 17
Inquiry Flipchart p. 4—Measure Up/Animal Models

Inquiry Lesson 4 How Do We Use Inquiry Skills? 27
Inquiry Flipchart p. 5—How Do We Use Inquiry Skills?

Lesson 5 How Do Scientists Work? 29
Inquiry Flipchart p. 6—Holding Water/My Fingerprints

People in Science: Mary Anderson 39

Unit 1 Review 41

Now I Get the Big Idea!

Science Notebook
Before you begin each lesson, be sure to write your thoughts about the Essential Question.

Essential Question

What Are Senses and Other Tools?

🧠 Engage Your Brain!

Find the answer to the question in the lesson.

What **sense** is this child trying <u>not</u> to use?

the sense of

_____

Active Reading

Lesson Vocabulary

1 Preview the lesson.

2 Write the two vocabulary terms here.

_____ _____

Your Senses

How do you learn about things?
You use your five senses. Your **senses**
are the way you learn about the world.
The senses are sight, hearing, smell, taste,
and touch. You use different body parts
for different senses.

Active Reading

The main idea is the most important idea about
something. Draw two lines under the main idea.

You hear with
your ears.

Learning with Your Senses

How can your senses help you learn?
Look at the pictures. What would your
senses tell you about each thing?

Touching

You touch to learn about
texture—how things feel.

Hearing

You listen to learn
how things sound.

▶ **Underline how you learn
how things feel.**

Seeing
You use sight to observe color, shape, and size.

Smelling
You use smell to learn how things smell.

Tasting
You taste to learn if foods are sweet, sour, or salty.

▶ **You use sight to observe three things. Circle the words.**

Tools to Explore

You can use science tools to learn more. People use **science tools** to find out about things.

A hand lens is a science tool. It helps you see small things. You could not see these things as well with just your eyes.

Active Reading

Find the sentence that tells about **science tools**. Draw a line under the sentence.

These children are using a hand lens to closely observe a flower.

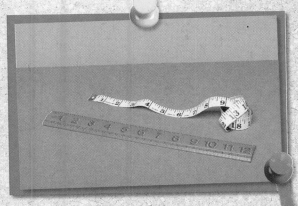

Ruler and Tape Measure

A ruler measures how long things are. A tape measure measures around things.

Measuring Cup

A measuring cup measures liquids.

Tools for Measuring

▶ Circle the names of tools you use to measure.

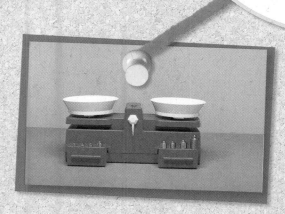

Balance

A balance compares how heavy things are.

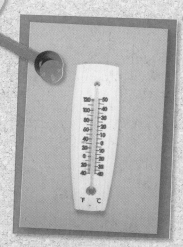

Thermometer

A thermometer measures temperature. It tells how hot and cold things are.

Measuring Up

What would happen if we used different things to measure the same object? We might get different measurements. With science tools, we get the same measurement each time.

This girl is using her shoes to measure the rug.

Do the Math!

Measure Length

Measure how long a bookcase is. Use a small shoe, a large shoe, and a tape measure or a ruler. The tape measure or ruler measures in feet.

How long is the bookcase when you measure

1. with a small shoe?

   about _____ small shoes long

2. with a big shoe?

   about _____ big shoes long

3. with a ruler or tape measure?

   about _____ feet long

Why should you use a ruler or a tape measure to measure the bookcase?

_____

_____

_____

_____

Sum It Up!

① Choose It!

Which tool is <u>not</u> used to measure? Mark an X on it.

② Circle It!

Which tool helps you observe small things? Circle it.

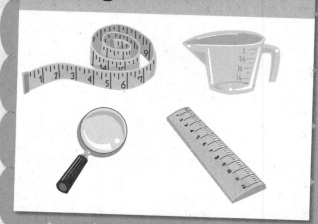

③ Match It!

Look at each thing. Which sense helps you learn about it? Draw lines to match them.

You touch to feel how furry something is.

You see to read.

You smell food baking.

Name _____

Word Play

You use different body parts for different senses. Label each body part with its sense.

| hearing | sight | smell | taste | touch |

Apply Concepts

Draw a line to the picture whose name completes the sentence.

1. Measure a ball with a _____.

2. Measure water with a _____.

3. Observe an ant with a _____.

4. Compare how heavy with a _____.

5. Measure length with a _____.

Take It Home!

Family Members: See *ScienceSaurus*® for more information about science tools.

Inquiry Flipchart p. 3

Name _____

How Can We Use Our Senses?

Set a Purpose

Tell what you want to find out.

_____

Think About the Procedure

❶ What will you observe?

_____

_____

❷ How will you find out the sound of breaking celery?

_____

Record Your Data

In this chart, record what you observe.

Sense	Observation
sight	
touch	
smell	
hear	
taste	

Draw Conclusions

What did you find out about celery? How do you know?

_____

_____

Ask More Questions

What other questions could you ask about celery and your senses?

_____

_____

Essential Question

What Are Inquiry Skills?

 **Engage Your Brain!**

Find the answer to the question in the lesson.

What can you infer this boy is doing?

The boy is

_____.

Active Reading

Lesson Vocabulary

❶ Preview the lesson.

❷ Write the vocabulary term here.

_____

Skills to Help You Learn

Observe and Compare

How can you be like a scientist? You can use inquiry skills. **Inquiry skills** help you find out information. They help you learn about your world.

Active Reading

You can compare things. You find ways they are alike. A child on this page is comparing two things. Draw a triangle around the two things.

Falling Leaves Forest

observe

compare

Predict and Measure

measure

predict

Rocky Cliff

Circle the inquiry skill that helps you find the size of an object.

19

Classify and Communicate

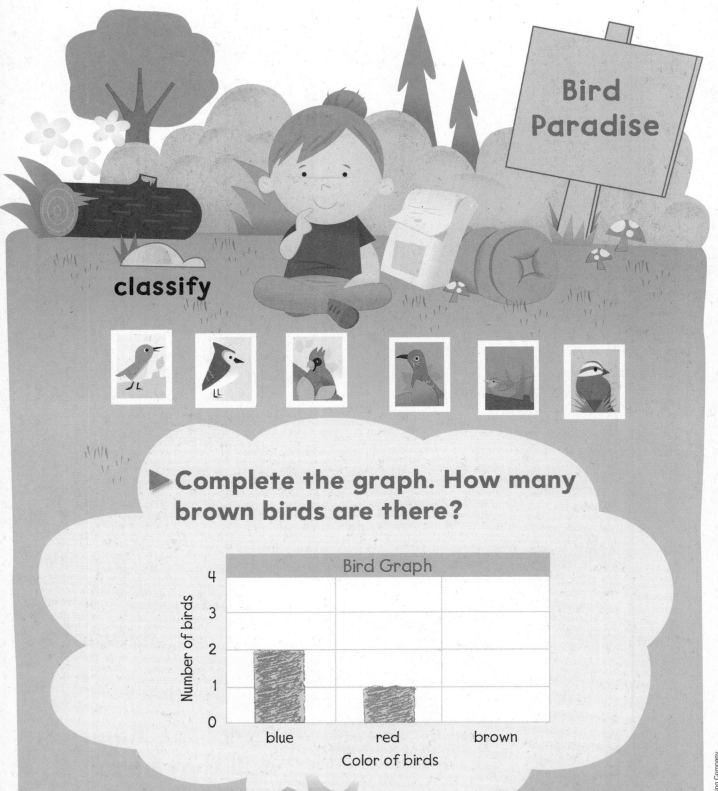

classify

► Complete the graph. How many brown birds are there?

Bird Graph

Number of birds

Color of birds

blue   red   brown

communicate

Hypothesize and Plan an Investigation

hypothesize

plan an investigation

Rolling Logs Hill

▶ Which child made a hypothesis? Draw a line under the hypothesis.

Infer and Draw Conclusions

I think the light container is empty.

Picnic Palace

infer

Empty containers are lighter than full containers.

draw conclusions

▶ Underline the conclusion the child drew.

Make a Model and Sequence

Butterfly Garden

▶ Things may happen in order.
Write 1 beside what happens first.
Write 2 beside what happens second.
Write 3 beside what happens third.
Write 4 beside what happens last.

make a model

sequence

Sum It Up!

1 Circle It!

You want to learn about something. Circle what you do to find out.

predict

classify

plan an investigation

2 Choose It!

What inquiry skill does this show?

communicate

make a model

sequence

3 Draw It!

Observe an object. Draw it. Tell about it.

This is a _____. It is _____.

Brain Check

Name _____

Word Play

Circle the letters to spell the words.
Then complete the sentence.

compare	classify	infer	measure
observe	predict	sequence	

```
s  e  s  e  q  u  e  n  c  e  a
v  c  l  a  s  s  i  f  y
u  l  r  i  n  f  e  r  t
r  m  e  a  s  u  r  e  p
o  b  s  e  r  v  e  g  e
e  w  p  r  e  d  i  c  t
c  o  m  p  a  r  e  t  z
```

All the words in the puzzle
are _____ .

Apply Concepts

Circle the word that matches the meaning.

① tell what you learn	communicate	observe
② sort things into groups	sequence	classify
③ tell how things are alike	make a model	compare
④ put things in order	sequence	hypothesize
⑤ find out how much or how long	measure	infer
⑥ use your senses	make a model	observe
⑦ make a good guess about what will happen	predict	sequence
⑧ decide what steps to follow	draw conclusions	plan an investigation

Family Members: Discuss with your child how inquiry skills are used around the home. For example, you measure when you cook, and classify when you sort laundry.

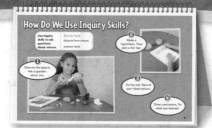

Inquiry Flipchart p. 5

Name _____

Essential Question

How Do We Use Inquiry Skills?

Set a Purpose

Tell what you want to find out.

_____

_____

_____

Think About the Procedure

❶ What fair test did you plan? Write your plan here.

_____

_____

❷ What science tools will you use for your test?

_____

27

Record Your Data

Draw or write. Record what you observe.

Draw Conclusions

What conclusions can you draw?

_____

_____

Ask More Questions

What other questions could you ask?

_____

_____

Essential Question

How Do Scientists Work?

🧠 Engage Your Brain!

Find the answer to the question in the lesson.

How do you paint a rainbow using only three colors of paint?

You can mix

_____

Active Reading

Lesson Vocabulary

1 Preview the lesson.

2 Write the vocabulary term here.

_____

Think Like a Scientist

Scientists plan an investigation when they want to learn more. An **investigation** is a test scientists do. There are different plans for investigations. Here is one plan.

Observe

First, observe something. Ask a question about it.

Active Reading

Clue words can help you find the order of things. **First** is a clue word. Draw a box around this clue word.

What would happen if we mixed yellow paint and blue paint?

© Houghton Mifflin Harcourt Publishing Company

Hypothesize and Make a Plan

Next, make a hypothesis. State something you can test. Plan a fair test to see whether you are correct.

My Hypothesis

Blue paint and yellow paint mix to make green.

My Plan

1. Put yellow paint on a plate.
2. Put blue paint on a plate.
3. Mix the paints.

▶ **Do you think yellow paint and blue paint mix to make green? Circle your answer.**

Yes   No

Do the Test

Do the test. Follow the steps of your plan. Observe what happens.

Active Reading

The main idea is the most important idea about something. Draw two lines under the main idea.

We can mix the paints to see what happens.

Draw Conclusions

Draw conclusions from your test. What did you learn? Compare your results with your classmates' results. What would happen if you did the test again? How do you know?

If we do the test again, yellow paint and blue paint will still make green.

▶ Circle the color that yellow and blue make when you mix them.

Record What You Observe

Scientists record what they learn from an investigation. You can keep a record in a science notebook. You can draw pictures. You can write.

Active Reading

A detail is a fact about a main idea. Draw one line under a detail. Draw an arrow to the main idea it tells about.

▶ **What colors make green?**

1 Write It!

You have a [feather] and a [block].
You will drop them.
You think the block will fall faster.
How can you test your idea?

_____

2 Circle It!

You do the steps in an investigation.
Now you draw what happens.
Which step are you doing?
Circle it.

Observe.   Plan a fair test.

Record what you observe.

 **Brain Check**

Name _____

Word Play

Unscramble the word to complete each sentence. Use these words if you need help.

observe	hypothesize	investigation	record

ntiovetigansi

❶ To learn more about something, you do an _____.

eyhtpoheszi

❷ When you make a statement you can test, you _____.

dreorc

❸ After you do a test, you should _____ your results.

beosver

❹ When you look at something closely, you _____ it.

Apply Concepts

Can air move a penny and a feather?
Tell how you could investigate.
Write a number from 1 to 5 to show the order.

_____ Write a plan.

_____ Ask a question–
Can air move a penny and a feather?

_____ Record what you observe.

_____ Share your results.

_____ Follow your plan.

Family Members: Ask your child to tell you about the steps of an investigation. Then plan an investigation you and your child can try at home.

Learn About...
Mary Anderson

In 1902, Mary Anderson observed something. In bad weather, drivers had trouble seeing. They had to drive with the window open. Or they had to get out to clean off the windshield. Anderson got an idea. She invented the windshield wiper.

Drivers could use it from inside their vehicle. They could see the road and stay warm and dry.

Fun Fact

By the 1920s all cars had windshield wipers.

This Leads to That

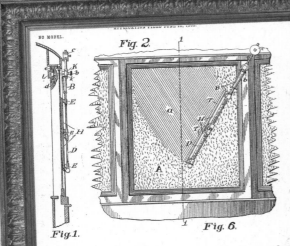

Mary Anderson invented the first windshield wiper. This shows an early drawing.

Robert Kearns invented a windshield wiper that went on and off as needed.

▶ **How does Mary Anderson's invention help people today?**

_____

_____

_____

Name _____

Vocabulary Review

Use the terms in the box to complete the sentences.

> inquiry skills
> investigation
> senses

1. You learn about the world by using your _____.

2. To find out information, you use _____.

3. To learn more, scientists plan an _____.

Science Concepts

Fill in the letter of the choice that best answers the question.

4. What can you learn from listening to music?
   - Ⓐ how it feels
   - Ⓑ how it looks
   - Ⓒ how it sounds

5. You want to find out which toy car goes a greater distance. What question do you ask?
   - Ⓐ Why do cars roll?
   - Ⓑ Which car is older?
   - Ⓒ Which car will roll farther?

6. Which sense is the boy using to observe the flower?

Ⓐ hearing
Ⓑ smell
Ⓒ taste

7. You do a fair test and draw the results. What are you doing?
Ⓐ classifying
Ⓑ communicating
Ⓒ measuring

8. You want to measure the length of a leaf. Which science tool will you use?

Ⓐ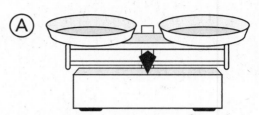

Ⓑ

Ⓒ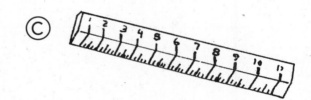

9. You tell what happens first, next, and last in an activity. Which inquiry skill is this?

Ⓐ hypothesize

Ⓑ infer

Ⓒ sequence

10. Which step in an investigation is shown?

Ⓐ doing a test

Ⓑ drawing a conclusion

Ⓒ recording results

11. What do you do when you classify?

Ⓐ group things by how they are alike

Ⓑ tell what you think will happen

Ⓒ use observations to tell why something happens

12. You and a classmate compare your results. The results are not the same. What should you do?

Ⓐ repeat the test

Ⓑ tell your teacher

Ⓒ throw away the results

Inquiry and the Big Idea
Write the answers to these questions.

13. Look at this picture.

a. What sense is the girl using?

_____

b. What can she learn by petting the dog?

_____

14. You want to investigate how fast two toy cars roll.
Your hypothesis is that a metal car rolls faster than
a wooden car. What steps would you follow to test
your hypothesis?

_____

_____

_____

Technology All Around Us

Big Idea

Engineers use a process to design and build something new. They use many different kinds of materials.

children's playground

I Wonder How

An engineer planned a design for this playground. How?
Turn the page to find out.

Here's How An engineer drew ideas on a plan. The plan had many fun things for kids.

In this unit, you will explore this Big Idea, the Essential Questions, and the Investigations on the Inquiry Flipchart.

© Houghton Mifflin Harcourt Publishing Company · (bkgd) © Wikkea/Shutterstock, Inc.; (border) © NDisc/Age Fotostock

Levels of Inquiry Key ■ DIRECTED ■ **GUIDED** ■ INDEPENDENT

Track Your Progress

Big Idea Engineers use a process to design and build something new. They use many different kinds of materials.

Essential Questions

Lesson 1 How Do Engineers Work? 47
Inquiry Flipchart p. 7—Don't Crack Up!/Make It Fly!

Inquiry Lesson 2 How Can We Solve a Problem? 59
Inquiry Flipchart p. 8—How Can We Solve a Problem?

Lesson 3 What Materials Make Up Objects? 61
Inquiry Flipchart p. 9—Build It!/Materials Mission

Inquiry Lesson 4 How Can Materials Be Sorted? 73
Inquiry Flipchart p. 10—How Can Materials Be Sorted?

People in Science: Dr. Eugene Tssui 75

Unit 2 Review 77

Now I Get the Big Idea!

Science Notebook

Before you begin each lesson, be sure to write your thoughts about the Essential Question.

Essential Question

How Do Engineers Work?

Engage Your Brain!

Find the answer to the question in the lesson.

How do you scratch an itch you cannot reach?

You can

_____

_____ .

Active Reading

Lesson Vocabulary

1 Preview the lesson.

2 Write the two vocabulary terms here.

_____   _____

Problem Solvers

An **engineer** uses math and science to solve everyday problems. Engineers work on many kinds of problems. Some engineers design robots. Others plan roads. Some design cars.

Active Reading

A detail is a fact about a main idea. Draw one line under a detail. Draw an arrow to the main idea it tells about.

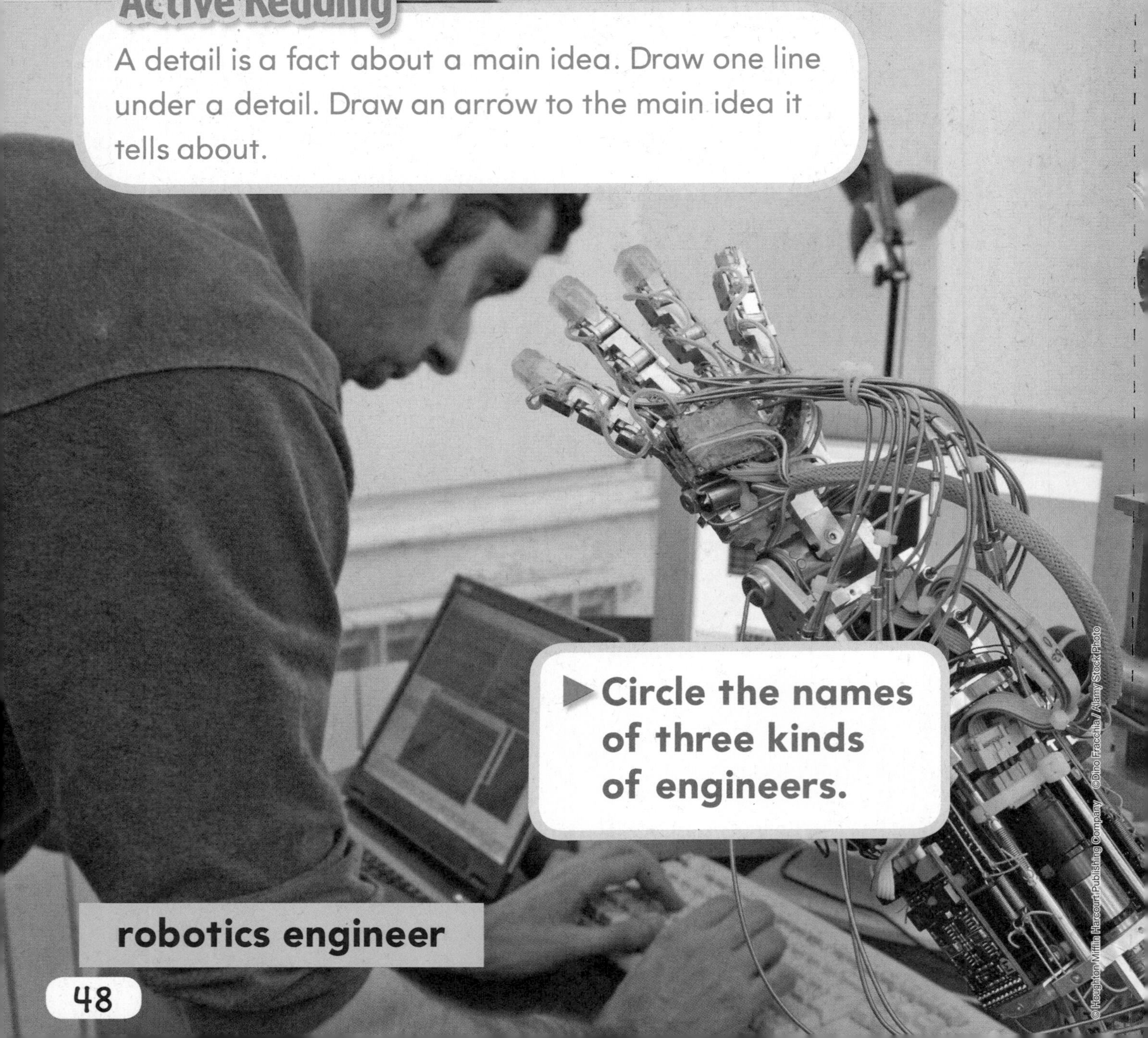

▶ **Circle the names of three kinds of engineers.**

robotics engineer

Engineers use a design process to solve problems. A **design process** is a plan with steps that help engineers find good solutions.

The Design Process

1. Find a Problem
2. Plan and Build
3. Test and Improve
4. Redesign
5. Communicate

mechanical engineer

civil engineer

The Design Process

Find a Problem

Jack has an itch he cannot reach. How can he scratch it? The steps of this design process show Jack what to do.

Jack names his problem. He needs to find a way to scratch his back. He brainstorms ways to solve his problem.

Jack tries to scratch his back.

▶ **What problem does Jack want to solve?**

_____

_____

Jack gets out his science notebook.
He wants to record what he does to solve
his problem.

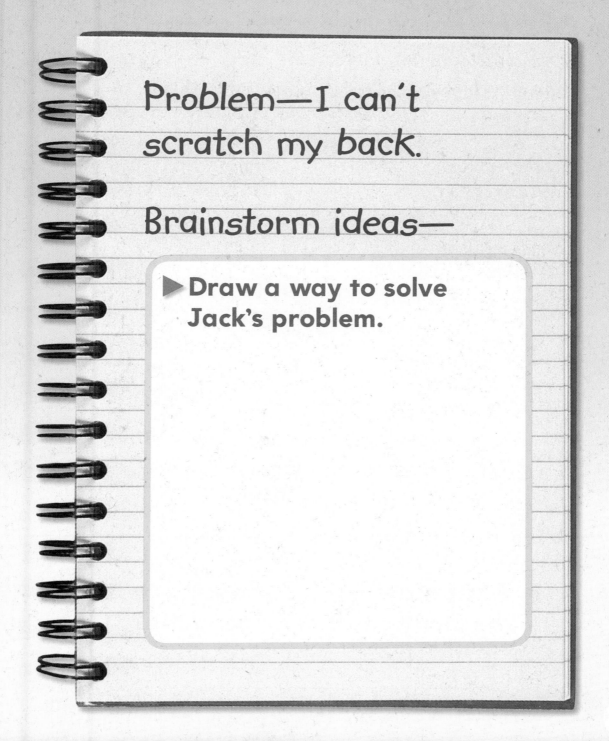

Problem—I can't scratch my back.

Brainstorm ideas—

▶ Draw a way to solve Jack's problem.

2 Plan and Build

Then Jack chooses a solution to try. He makes a plan. Jack draws and labels his plan. He chooses the best materials to use.

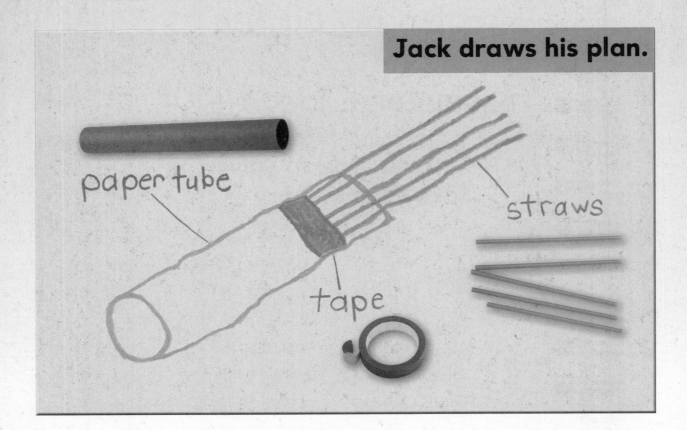

Jack draws his plan.

paper tube

straws

tape

▶ **What material is Jack using to hold the straws to the paper tube?**

_____

52

Jack builds his back scratcher.
He uses the materials he chose and the
plan he made.

Jack makes his
back scratcher.

Jack tests the back scratcher with a friend. They try the back scratcher to see whether it works. Does the back scratcher solve the problem?

▶ **Write a way to improve the design of the back scratcher.**

_____

_____

Jack and a friend test the back scratcher.

4 Redesign

Jack thinks of a way to redesign his back scratcher. He adds notes about how to make it better.

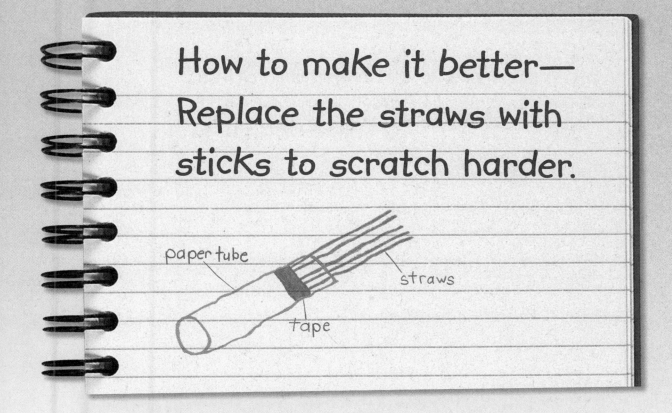

How to make it better—
Replace the straws with
sticks to scratch harder.

paper tube

straws

tape

5 Communicate

Jack writes and draws to show what happened. He can share what he learned with others.

▶ **Which material is Jack using to make his design better? Circle the word.**

Sum It Up!

① Circle It!

Circle the step of the design process shown in the picture.

How to make it better—
Replace the straws with
sticks to scratch harder.

paper tube

straws

tape

Find a Problem

Plan and Build

Redesign

② Solve It!

Answer the riddle.

I solve problems using
science and math.
The design process leads
me along the right path.

Who am I?

_____

Brain Check

Name _____

Word Play

Write a label for each picture.

| choose materials | build | engineer | test |

_____

_____

_____

_____

Apply Concepts

Write numbers to put the steps of the design process in order. The first one is done for you.

The Design Process

_____ Test and Improve

___1___ Find a Problem

_____ Communicate

_____ Redesign

_____ Plan and Build

Family Members: See *ScienceSaurus*® for more information about the design process.

Inquiry Flipchart p. 8

Name _____

Essential Question

How Can We Solve a Problem?

Set a Purpose

Tell what you will do.

_____

_____

Think About the Procedure

1 What steps will you follow to build your stand?

_____

_____

2 How will you know that your stand works?

_____

Record Your Data

Draw and label a picture that shows what happened.

Draw Conclusions

How did your solution work? How could you redesign the stand to make it better?

_____

_____

Ask More Questions

What other questions could you ask about designing a solution to a problem?

_____

Essential Question

What Materials Make Up Objects?

Engage Your Brain!

Find the answer to the question in the lesson.

What could you make with this wood?

_____

Active Reading

Lesson Vocabulary

1 Preview the lesson.

2 Write the three vocabulary terms here.

_____   _____

_____

Play Your Part

Objects may be made of different parts. The parts go together to make the whole.

Look at this bicycle. It has wheels, a frame, and other parts. These parts go together to make a bicycle.

Active Reading

A detail is a fact about a main idea. Draw a line under a detail. Draw an arrow to the main idea it tells about.

_____

_____ wheel _____

_____

▶ Write labels for the parts of the bicycle.

bicycle

A Material World

Look at this house. One part is brick. Another part is metal. Other parts are wood. The windows are glass.

Brick, metal, wood, and glass are materials. **Materials** are what objects are made of.

Active Reading

Find the sentence that tells the meaning of **materials**. Draw a line under the sentence.

brick

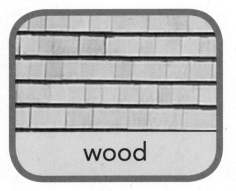
wood

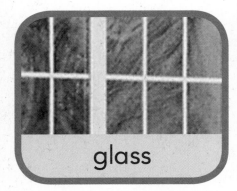
glass

metal

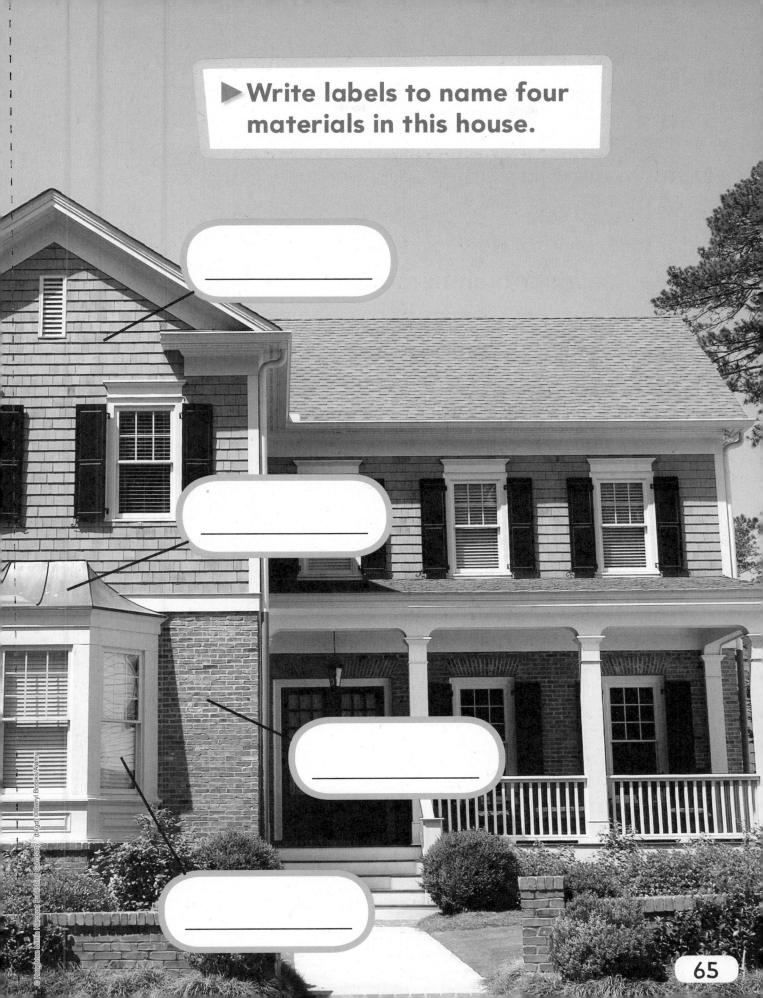

► Write labels to name four materials in this house.

_____

_____

_____

_____

Made to Order

Materials are natural or human-made. **Natural** materials are found in nature. For example, cotton is from a plant. Wood is from trees. Metal is in rocks.

People make **human-made** materials such as plastics and nylon. Scientists first made them in a lab. Scientists changed petroleum into these new materials not found in nature.

trees

cotton

Crude Oil

petroleum

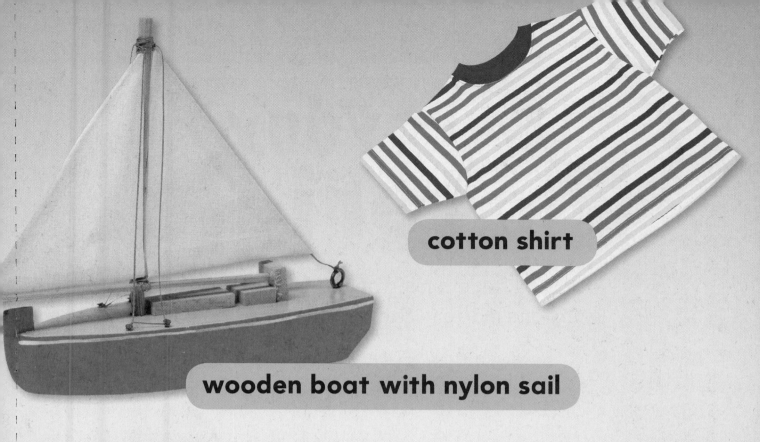

cotton shirt

wooden boat with nylon sail

Some objects are made of natural materials. Others are made of human-made materials. Some objects are made of both natural and human-made materials.

▶ **Mark an X on the object made from both natural and human-made materials.**

plastic toys

Everyday Materials

Do you have a pair of jeans? Cotton jeans are made in factories. Here is how.

Active Reading

Things may happen in order. Draw a line under the step that happens first.

1

Looms weave cotton into cloth.

2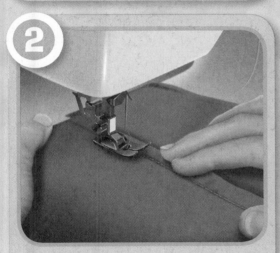

Workers use machines to cut and sew the cloth.

3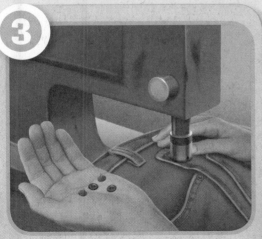

Workers use machines to put on metal rivets.

4 Now the jeans are ready to wear!

Sum It Up!

① Draw It!

Draw something made of glass on the house.

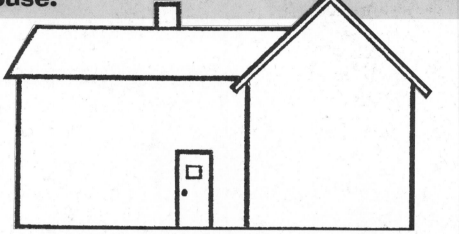

② Match It!

Draw a line to match each toy with the kind of material it is made from.

human-made   natural   both

Name _____

Word Play

Color the letters to spell the vocabulary words.
Write the words to complete the sentences.

| human-made | materials | natural |

n	a	t	u	r	a	l	t	w	k
c	t	o	w	r	e	g	y	p	s
h	u	m	a	n	m	a	d	e	y
g	m	a	t	e	r	i	a	l	s
k	n	y	u	o	s	d	x	p	m

1 Objects are made of _____.

2 Materials made in a lab are _____.

3 Materials found in nature are _____.

Apply Concepts

Complete the chart. Name and classify the materials each object is made from.

Materials Chart

Object	Material	Natural, human-made, or both
①	_____ _____	_____
②	_____ _____	_____
③	_____ _____	_____

Name _____

Essential Question

How Can Materials Be Sorted?

Set a Purpose

Tell what you want to do.

_____

Think About the Procedure

1 What will you observe about the objects?

_____

_____

2 How will you sort the objects?

_____

_____

Record Your Data

Draw or write to show how you sorted the objects.

Natural	Human-made	Both

Draw Conclusions

How could you tell what objects were made of?

_____

_____

Ask More Questions

What other questions could you ask about objects and materials?

_____

_____

_____

© Houghton Mifflin Harcourt Publishing Company

Get to Know
Dr. Eugene Tssui

Dr. Eugene Tssui is an architect. This is a kind of engineer. An architect designs homes and other buildings.

Dr. Tssui studies forms in nature, such as sea shells. He bases his designs on what he learns. Dr. Tssui says that nature is our great teacher.

Fun Fact

Dr. Tssui also designs his own clothes.

Dr. Tssui's Designs

▶ Draw a line from each building to the natural form it is based on.

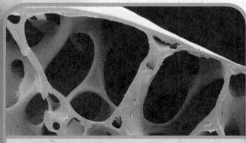
the bones of a bird

fish scales

dragonfly wings

▶ Think about a form from nature. Use it to design your own building.

Unit 2 Review

Name _____

Vocabulary Review

Use the terms in the box to complete the sentences.

> engineer
>
> materials
>
> natural

1. Someone who uses math and science to solve everyday problems is an _____.

2. An object is made of its _____.

3. Something that is made from things found in nature is _____.

Science Concepts

Fill in the letter of the choice that best answers the question.

4. A cotton shirt has a metal zipper. What kinds of materials make up the shirt?

   Ⓐ natural

   Ⓑ human-made

   Ⓒ both natural and human-made

5. Loveleen wants to build a feeder that many birds can use. How can she follow the design process?

   Ⓐ buy a new bird feeder

   Ⓑ plan and build a solution

   Ⓒ tell a friend about the feeder

6. Cara is playing with two toys.

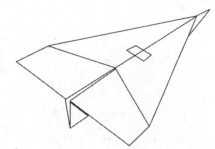

Which toy is made from a human-made material?

Ⓐ the paper airplane

Ⓑ the plastic bucket

Ⓒ both are made from human-made materials

7. Which is **true** of all engineers?

Ⓐ All engineers build roads.

Ⓑ All engineers design cars.

Ⓒ All engineers solve problems.

8. Which object is made from natural materials?

Ⓐ a nylon shirt

Ⓑ a plastic bottle

Ⓒ a wood table

9. What is the **first** step of the design process?

Ⓐ Find a Problem

Ⓑ Plan and Build

Ⓒ Test and Improve

10. A river is between two towns. People want to drive from one town to the other. Two engineers talk about the problem.

How do they plan to solve it?

Ⓐ build a tunnel under the river

Ⓑ build a bridge over the river

Ⓒ give boats to the people in the towns

11. You draw a picture of something you designed.

What step of the design process is this?

Ⓐ Communicate

Ⓑ Redesign

Ⓒ Test and Improve

12. Which object is made of both natural materials and human-made materials?

Ⓐ a metal bucket with a wooden handle

Ⓑ a wood door with a metal handle

Ⓒ a cotton bag with a plastic handle

Inquiry and the Big Idea
Write the answers to these questions.

13. Geeta sorted objects into these two groups.

Group 1	Group 2
wood pencil	plastic toy
sheet of paper	nylon jacket

a. How did she sort the objects?

_____

_____

b. Name one thing that could be added to each group.

_____

14. Cold air is coming in under Michael's door. He wants to use the design process to find a solution.

a. What should Michael do first?

_____

b. Michael builds a tool. How can he test it?

_____

c. What should he do if the tool does not work?

_____

UNIT 3
Weather and Seasons

Big Idea

Weather changes from day to day and from season to season. You can use different tools to measure weather.

▶ S1E1., S1E1.a, S1E1.b, S1E1.c, S1E1.d

winter weather

I Wonder Why
Icicles form in winter. Why?
Turn the page to find out.

Here's Why Air in the winter is cold. Cold air causes liquid water to freeze into a solid.

In this unit, you will explore this Big Idea, the Essential Questions, and the Investigations on the Inquiry Flipchart.

Levels of Inquiry Key ■ DIRECTED ■ GUIDED ■ INDEPENDENT

Track Your Progress

Big Idea Weather changes from day to day and from season to season. You can use different tools to measure weather.

Essential Questions

✓ **Lesson 1 What Is Weather?** 83
   Inquiry Flipchart p. 11—Hot or Cold?/Make a Pinwheel
   S1E1.b

○ **Inquiry Lesson 2 What Can We Observe About Weather?** 97
   Inquiry Flipchart p. 12—What Can We Observe About Weather?
   S1E1.a, S1E1.c

○ **People in Science:** June Bacon-Bercey. 101

○ **Lesson 3 What Are Seasons?** 103
   Inquiry Flipchart p. 13—Keeping Warm/Turn Over a New Leaf
   S1E1.d

○ **S.T.E.M. Engineering and Technology:** Weather Wisdom 115
   Inquiry Flipchart p. 14—Build It: Rain Gauge
   S1E1.c

○ **Unit 3 Review** 117

○ **Now I Get the Big Idea!**

Science Notebook

Before you begin each lesson, be sure to write your thoughts about the Essential Question.

Essential Question

What Is Weather?

🧠 Engage Your Brain!

Find the answer to the question in the lesson.

Rainbows usually follow rainy weather. Which tool could you use to measure rainfall?

_____

Active Reading

Lesson Vocabulary

1 Preview the lesson.

2 Write the four vocabulary terms here.

_____ _____

_____ _____

Weather Watch

Look outside. Is the sun out? Is the air warm or cool? Are there any clouds? Do you feel any wind? **Wind** is air that moves.

Weather is what the air outside is like. Weather may change during the day. It may also change from day to day and from month to month.

Active Reading

A detail is a fact about a main idea. Draw one line under a detail. Draw an arrow to the main idea the detail tells about.

Is it cloudy or sunny?

Is it windy or calm?

Is it hot or cold?

Is it rainy or icy?

Is it cloudy or clear?

▶ Circle the word that tells about the weather in each picture.

Measure It!

You can use tools to measure weather. A thermometer is a tool that measures temperature. **Temperature** is the measure of how hot or cold something is. Temperature is measured in degrees.

Active Reading

Find the sentence that tells the meaning of **temperature**. Draw a line under the sentence.

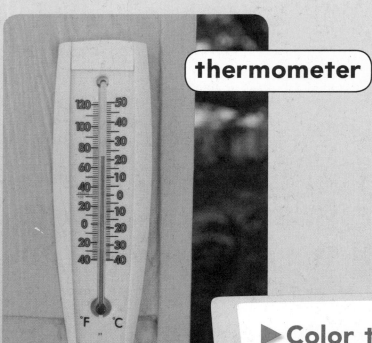

thermometer

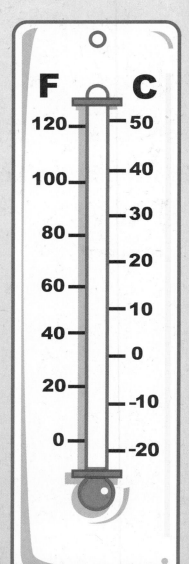

▶ **Color the thermometer to show 80 °F.**

Rain is a form of water that falls from the sky. A rain gauge is a tool that measures how much water falls.

rain gauge

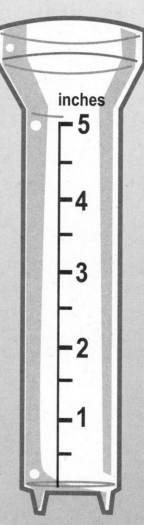

inches

5

4

3

2

1

▶Color the rain gauge to show that 3 inches of rain fell.

Precipitation

Rain

There are different kinds of wet weather. **Precipitation** is water that falls from the clouds toward the ground. Did you know that clouds are made up of water droplets or bits of ice? Clouds can be a mixture of both, too!

Precipitation can be a liquid or a solid. Rain is a liquid. It falls in drops from the clouds.

▶ **Draw objects that the girl might use so she does not get wet.**

Snow

Another kind of precipitation is called snow. Snow is a solid. Bits of frozen water called ice crystals form to make snowflakes. Snowflakes fall to the ground in cold weather.

▶ **What are questions you can ask about rain and snow?**

_____

_____

_____

_____

Snowflakes have many different shapes.

Sleet

Sometimes rain freezes before it reaches the ground and changes into sleet. This happens when raindrops fall into a layer of cold air. The raindrops freeze into solids. Sleet is sometimes called ice pellets. These tiny bits of ice bounce when they hit the ground.

Active Reading

A detail is a fact about a main idea. Draw one line under a detail. Draw an arrow to the main idea it tells about.

Hailstones

Hailstones are frozen balls or lumps of ice. They form in clouds when raindrops are in very cold air. Hailstones fall to the ground during thunderstorms and in warm weather. Some hailstones can be as big as softballs!

Hailstones can cause damage to cars and homes.

▶ **What are questions you can ask about sleet and hailstones?**

_____

_____

_____

Predict It!

Scientists observe and track weather over time. They look for changes in weather. They use tools to learn what the weather may be. Scientists use what they learn to make a weather report. A weather report helps people. They can get ready for the coming weather.

weather satellite

Do the Math!
Compare Numbers

Monday	Tuesday	Wednesday

50 °F	40 °F	45 °F

We use these tools to observe and track weather.

weather station

weather balloon

Look at the temperatures on the left.
Write one of them in the empty box below.
Write >, <, or = to compare the two numbers.

| 45 °F | ◯ | _____ °F |

Sum It Up!

① Draw It!

Draw two pictures. Show solid precipitation in one box. Show liquid precipitation in the other. Label each picture.

_____   _____

② Solve It!

Write a weather word to solve.

I fall to the ground during a thunderstorm. I can be as big as a softball.

I am _____.

③ Match It!

Match the words to the pictures.

rain gauge

thermometer

Word Play

Write a word from the box for each clue.

wind	thermometer	temperature

a measure of how hot or cold something is

— (4) — — — — (3) — — — (6)

air that is moving

— (1) — — —

a tool used to measure temperature

— (5) — — — — (2) — — (7)

Solve the riddle. Write the circled letters in order on the lines below.

I am what the air outside is like.
What am I?

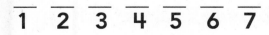 ___ ___ ___ ___ ___ ___ ___
1   2   3   4   5   6   7

Apply Concepts

Write a word from the box to fill in the blanks.

| cold | rainy | sunny | hot |

Observation	Inference
Children are swimming in the lake.	The day is _____.
The trees are moving back and forth.	The day is _____.
People are using umbrellas.	The day is _____.
People are wearing sunglasses.	The day is _____.

Take It Home!

Inquiry Flipchart p. 12

Lesson 2
INQUIRY

S1E1.a Types of weather;
S1E1.c Weather conditions and
weather data

Name _____

Essential Question

What Can We Observe About Weather?

Set a Purpose

Tell what you want to find out.

_____

_____

Think About the Procedure

❶ When will you observe the weather?

_____

_____

❷ What will you observe?

_____

_____

Record Your Data

Glue picture cards into the chart to show the weather.
You can use a calendar to record the weather, too.

Weather This Week

Monday	Tuesday	Wednesday	Thursday	Friday

Draw Conclusions

How is the weather alike from day to day?
How is the weather different from day to day?

_____

_____

How did you make your prediction?

_____

Ask More Questions

What other questions could you ask about the weather?

_____

Picture Cards

Cut out the weather cards on the dashed lines.

clear	clear	clear	clear	clear
cloudy	cloudy	cloudy	cloudy	cloudy
rainy	rainy	rainy	rainy	rainy
icy	icy	icy	icy	icy
hot	hot	hot	hot	hot
cold	cold	cold	cold	cold
windy	windy	windy	windy	windy

4 Things to Know About June Bacon-Bercey

1 June Bacon-Bercey is a meteorologist.

2 She was the first female meteorologist on television.

3 She won money, which she used to help other women become meteorologists.

4 She enjoys teaching.

Word Whiz

▶ Learn weather words. Find the words in the word search below. Draw a circle around each word you find.

tornado   hurricane   lightning   thunder   storm   blizzard

l i g h t n i n g q
w m r n o t b y v h
b d l z r x s p c u
l t h u n d e r b r
i j g s a y z q m r
z q f g d g f d s i
z w s t o r m h j c
a r d k y y p l k a
r t s h p q w r t n
d y p f j s d c b e

Essential Question

What Are Seasons?

Engage Your Brain!

Find the answer to the question in the lesson.

In which season do many trees have no leaves?

_____

Active Reading

Lesson Vocabulary

1 Preview the lesson.

2 Write the two vocabulary terms here.

_____   _____

Spring Into Spring

A **season** is a time of year. Spring, summer, fall, and winter are the four seasons. They form a repeating pattern.

The weather changes with each season. These changes form a weather pattern. A **weather pattern** is a change in the weather that repeats.

Active Reading

Find the sentence that tells the meaning of **season**. Draw a line under the sentence.

People plant flowers in spring.

In spring, the air warms. There may be many rainy days. Plants begin to grow. Trees grow new leaves. People can wear light jackets outside.

▶ Circle the adult that has its young in spring.

Some animals have their young in spring.

Sunny Summer

Summer is the season that follows spring. In summer, the air can be hot. Some places may have storms. There are more hours of daylight than in spring.

Some plants grow fruit in summer. Young animals grow bigger. People dress to stay cool. They wear hats and sunglasses to keep safe from the sun.

▶ **Draw an object on the adult that would keep him safe from the sun.**

People canoe in summer.

▶ Draw to show how most trees look in summer.

This hare's fur is brown in summer. The brown fur helps the hare hide.

Fall Into Fall

Fall is the season that follows summer. The air gets cooler. There are fewer hours of daylight than in summer.

Some leaves change color and drop off the trees. Some animals move to warmer places. People wear jackets to stay warm.

Active Reading

A detail is a fact about a main idea. Draw one line under a detail. Draw an arrow to the main idea it tells about.

People rake leaves in fall.

▶ Draw to show how some trees look in fall.

Some animals gather food to store in winter.

Winter Weather

Winter is the season that follows fall. In some places, the air can be cold. It may even snow. Winter has the fewest hours of daylight.

Many trees lose their leaves in winter. Some animals grow more fur to keep warm. People wear warm coats outside. In a few months, it will be spring again.

▶ **Draw winter clothes on the person not dressed for the season.**

People play in the snow in winter.

▶ Draw to show how most trees look in winter.

The hare's fur has turned white. The hare can hide in the snow.

Sum It Up!

① Solve It!

Write the word that solves the riddle.

I am a time when trees have lots of leaves, or no leaves at all.

I am winter, spring, summer, or fall.

I am a _____ .

② Draw It!

Draw an activity you can do in spring.

③ Match It!

Match each word to the picture it tells about.

summer   winter   fall

Brain Check

Word Play

Name _____

Use the words below to complete the puzzle.

| season | weather pattern | winter |
| spring | summer | fall |

Across

1. the season that follows fall

2. the season that follows spring

3. the season that follows summer

4. a time of year

Down

5. the season that follows winter

6. a change in the weather that repeats

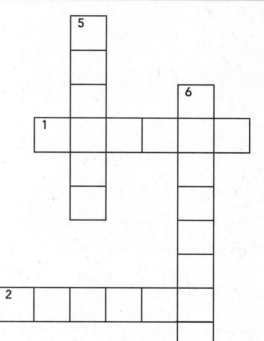

Apply Concepts

Cross out the things that do <u>not</u> belong in each picture.

Take It Home!

Family Members: Plan out family activities for the four seasons. Discuss with your child how the weather affects what you do and what you wear.

Weather Wisdom

Weather Tools

People use many tools to observe and record weather. The tools have changed over time. Weather vanes are older tools. Weather satellites are newer tools.

A thermometer measures temperature.

A weather satellite records weather from space.

A weather vane tells the direction of the wind.

A weather plane records weather from the sky.

S.T.E.M.
continued

Weather Tool Timeline

Use the timeline to answer
the questions.

1. Which is the oldest weather tool? Circle it.

2. Which is the newest weather tool?
   Draw a box around it.

3. Which tool came after the thermometer?
   Draw an X over it.

Build On It!

Design and build your own rain gauge. Complete
Build It: Rain Gauge on the Inquiry Flipchart.

Unit 3 Review

Vocabulary Review

Use the terms in the box to complete the sentences.

> season
> precipitation
> weather

1. What the air outside is like is called _____.

2. A time of year is a _____.

3. Water that falls to the ground as a solid or liquid is called _____.

Science Concepts

Fill in the letter of the choice that best answers the question.

4. What tool do you use to record the temperature each day?
   Ⓐ a rain gauge
   Ⓑ a thermometer
   Ⓒ a weather vane

5. You see dark clouds in the sky. What kind of weather is **most likely** coming?
   Ⓐ cold weather
   Ⓑ rainy weather
   Ⓒ sunny weather

6. In which season was this young lamb born?

Ⓐ fall
Ⓑ spring
Ⓒ summer

7. The Han family is ice skating outside. They are wearing heavy jackets. What season is it?

Ⓐ spring
Ⓑ summer
Ⓒ winter

8. How is fall **different** from spring?

Ⓐ Fall is a season.
Ⓑ People may wear jackets in spring.
Ⓒ Many trees lose their leaves in fall.

9. What does a rain gauge measure?

Ⓐ the direction of the wind
Ⓑ how much rain has fallen
Ⓒ the temperature of the air

10. Look at this picture.
What is the weather like?

Ⓐ clear and cold
Ⓑ cold and snowy
Ⓒ windy and warm

11. What is wind?
Ⓐ moving air
Ⓑ water from the sky
Ⓒ a tool for measuring
temperature

12. Look at what the
children are doing.

Which season is it?
Ⓐ fall
Ⓑ spring
Ⓒ summer

Inquiry and the Big Idea
Write the answers to these questions.

13. Look at the picture.

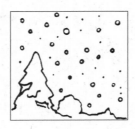

  a. What kind of precipitation do you see? Is it a solid or a liquid?

  _____

  b. What might you wear on a day like this?

  _____

  c. What might you do on a day like this?

  _____

14. Look at the tree.

  a. What season is it? How do you know?

  _____

  b. Which season comes next?

  _____

UNIT 4
Light and Sound

> **Big Idea**
>
> Light is energy that helps us see. Sound is energy that we hear.
>
> 🔶 S1P1, S1P1.a, S1P1.b, S1P1.c, S1P1.d, S1P1.e

I Wonder Why

This police car has a siren and flashing lights. Why?
Turn the page to find out.

UNIT 4

Here's Why The police car has a siren and flashing lights so people hear and see it, and then move out of the way.

In this unit, you will explore this Big Idea, the Essential Questions, and the Investigations on the Inquiry Flipchart.

Levels of Inquiry Key ■ DIRECTED ■ GUIDED ■ INDEPENDENT

Track Your Progress

Big Idea Light is energy that helps us see. Sound is energy that we hear.

Essential Questions

Lesson 1 What Is Light? 123
Inquiry Flipchart p. 15—No Light, No Sight!/Light It Up
S1P1.a; S1P1.b

Lesson 2 What Can We Learn About Shadows? 131
Inquiry Flipchart p. 16—What Can We Learn About Shadows?
S1P1.c

Lesson 3 What Is Sound? 133
Inquiry Flipchart p. 17—Water Music/Sound the Drum
S1P1.d

Inquiry Lesson 4 How Do We Make Sound? 143
Inquiry Flipchart p. 18—How Do We Make Sound?

S.T.E.M. **Engineering and Technology:**
Call Me! Telephone Timeline 145
Inquiry Flipchart p. 19—Design It: Make a Musical Instrument

Lesson 5 How Can We Use Light and Sound? 147
Inquiry Flipchart p. 20—Light or Sound?/An Emergency Alert
S1P1.e

🎓 **Careers in Science:** Ask a Piano Tuner 155

Unit 4 Review 157

Now I Get the Big Idea!

Science Notebook

Before you begin each lesson, be sure to write your thoughts about the Essential Question.

© Houghton Mifflin Harcourt Publishing Company (b) ©Candid Studio Inc./Corbis; (inset) ©Pete Ryan/National Geographic/Getty Images

Essential Question

What Is Light?

🧠 Engage Your Brain!

Find the answer to the question in the lesson.

Why does this stadium have lights?

This stadium has lights _____

_____

_____

Active Reading

Lesson Vocabulary

1 Preview the lesson.

2 Write the two vocabulary terms here.

_____ _____

Light All Around

Something that can do work and cause change has **energy**. Look around. What do you see? The sun makes its own light. **Light** is energy that lets you see. You can see objects when light shines on them.

We use light from the sun. We need it to play outdoors or read a book.

Active Reading

Find the sentence that tells the meaning of **light**. Draw a line under the sentence.

Other objects give off light to help us see. Do you like to go camping? Flashlights and headlamps help us see where we are walking at night. They light up dark places. Then we won't step on a rock or in a puddle!

Adults build a campfire. The light from the fire helps us see each other. The heat from the fire keeps us warm, too!

Active Reading

Underline words that name things that give us light.
Circle things in the picture that give us light.

Shed Some Light!

Light helps us to see objects when it is dark.

Cars have headlights. Drivers use them to see stop signs, people, and other cars. Street lights help us see where we are walking. They keep us safe.

We use lights in our homes, too. Electric lamps help us see in the dark. We turn them on when we eat dinner or play games. The light lets us see so we don't bump into objects.

Look at the pictures. Ask questions about the lights you see.

_____

_____

_____

_____

Sum It Up!

① Mark It!

Circle something that gives off light when it is dark outside.
Draw an X on something that helps you see in your house.

② Solve It!

Write the answer to the riddle on the line.

I crackle when I'm hot.
I keep you warm at night.
You build me when you camp.
I give you lots of light!
What am I?

_____

③ Draw It!

Draw a kind of light you use that helps you see things when it is dark.

128

 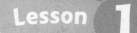

Name _____

Word Play

Unscramble the words. Then use each word in a sentence. Tell how each object gives you light to do an activity.

campfire	headlights	lamp	flashlight	sun

1. tisfalhglh ___ ___ ___ ___ ___ ___ ___ ___ ___ ___

_____

_____

2. plma ___ ___ ___ ___

_____

_____

3. nsu ___ ___ ___

_____

_____

4. apiecmfr ___ ___ ___ ___ ___ ___ ___ ___

_____

_____

5. haslgtedih ___ ___ ___ ___ ___ ___ ___ ___ ___ ___

_____

_____

Apply Concepts

Draw a line to the word and picture that complete the sentence.

1 We use a _____ to walk around a campsite at night.

sun

2 We use _____ when we drive a car at night.

streetlight

3 We use the _____ when we play outside during the day.

flashlight

4 We use a _____ when we walk on a sidewalk at night.

headlights

Name _____

Essential Question

What Can We Learn About Shadows?

Set a Purpose
Tell what you want to find out.

_____

_____

Think About the Procedure

1 How will I make a shadow?

_____

_____

2 How will you know how the shadow changes?

_____

_____

Record Your Data

Write about how the shadow changes in the chart.

How the Shadow Changes

Close to the wall	One step toward the light source	Two steps toward the light source

Draw Conclusions

How did the shadow change when you asked your friend to move closer to the light source?

_____

When is the shadow the biggest?

_____

Why do you think the shadow changed?

_____

_____

Ask More Questions

What other questions can you ask about shadows?

_____

_____

Essential Question

What Is Sound?

🧠 **Engage Your Brain!**

Find the answer to the question in the lesson.

What kind of sound does a marching band make?

a _____ sound

Active Reading

Lesson Vocabulary

1 Preview the lesson.

2 Write the four vocabulary terms here.

_____ _____

_____ _____

Sounds All Around

Listen. What do you hear? Is it a person talking? Is it a pencil tapping? Both are sounds. **Sound** is a kind of energy you hear.

Active Reading

Find the sentence that tells the meaning of **sound**. Draw a line under the sentence.

Sound is made when an object vibrates.
To **vibrate** is to move quickly back and forth.

The strings on a guitar vibrate and make sounds when you pluck them.

The top of a drum vibrates and makes a sound when you hit it.

▶ **Touch your throat and hum. What happens?**

it vibrates

Loud or Soft

Some sounds are loud. Other sounds are soft. **Loudness** is how loud or soft a sound is. A loud sound can make you cover your ears. A soft sound can be hard to hear.

Active Reading

When things are contrasted, you find out ways they are different. Draw triangles around two things that are being contrasted.

An instrument can make a loud or a soft sound. Its loudness changes with how you play it. A drum makes a louder sound if you hit it harder.

high pitch

low pitch

Some sounds are high. Some sounds are low. Pitch is how high or low a sound is.

▶**Look at the xylophone.**
1. Which bars have a low pitch?

the _____ bars

2. Which bars have a high pitch?

the _____ bars

Listen Up!

Sound is important to everyday life. Some sounds give you information. People talk to each other to learn things. A dog's bark may let you know that a person is coming. Sounds can warn you, too. A smoke detector warns of a fire.

What do these sounds tell you?

▶ **Draw an X on the picture that tells you someone is at the door.**

Sum It Up!

① Mark It!

Circle the place where people are quiet.
Draw an X on the place where people are loud.

② Choose It!

Circle the bell with a higher pitch.

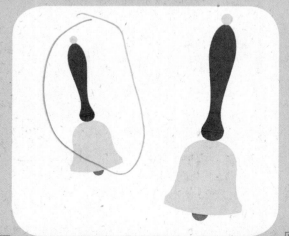

③ Draw It!

Draw an object that makes a warning sound.

Fire

Inquiry Flipchart p. 18

Name _____

Essential Question

How Do We Make Sound?

Set a Purpose

Tell what you want to do.

_____

_____

Think About the Procedure

1 How will you use your telephone?

_____

_____

2 What will you do with the string as you talk?

_____

Record Your Data

Write in the chart to tell what you heard.

How We Held the String	What We Heard
tight	
loose	

Draw Conclusions

What did you infer would happen when you held the string loose? Why do you think the sound changed?

_____

_____

_____

Ask More Questions

What other questions could you ask about the string telephone?

_____

_____

Call Me!

Telephone Timeline

How do you share news with a friend who lives far away? You can use a phone to call. Or, you can send a text. Phones were different long ago. Look at the timeline. It shows how phones have changed.

You used your finger to dial each number on this phone. It was easier to hear your friend. The phone had three parts: A receiver, a base, and a cord.

The first phone looked like this. First, you talked to an operator. Next, the operator connected you to your friend. Sometimes, it was hard to hear.

This phone had a base but not a cord. You could walk around the house while talking. You could make the volume louder.

How is your phone similar? How it is different?

_____

_____

145

S.T.E.M.
continued

Phones in the Future

Look at the phones today. They can do many things. Draw a picture. Show what a phone might look like in the future. Then write about new things this phone can do for you!

_____

_____

Build On It!

Make your own sounds! Complete **Make a Musical Instrument** on the Inquiry Flipchart.

Essential Question

How Can We Use Light and Sound?

🧠 Engage Your Brain!

Find the answer to the question in the lesson.

What are two things you can use as a signal to warn people of an emergency?

_____ and _____

Active Reading

Lesson Vocabulary

1 Preview the lesson.

2 Write the three vocabulary terms here.

_____   _____

_____   _____

In Case of Emergency

FIRE

What happens if there is a fire at your school? An alarm beeps loudly. It is an **alert** or warning. It is time to **evacuate** and leave your classroom. You hear a siren and see flashing lights. Both signals let you know help is coming!

Active Reading

Find the sentence that tells the meaning of **alert**. Draw a line under the sentence.

Sometimes we get an alert on a cell phone. It beeps loudly or vibrates. A message pops up on the screen. It tells us what to do.

A loud siren sounds when a tornado is coming. A **tornado** is a very strong wind. It comes down from clouds in the shape of a funnel. The alert lets us know to move to a safe place.

Tornado
warning
in your area
until 2 p.m.
Go to a
shelter now.

▶ **How does a cell phone alert you of an emergency?**

_____

_____

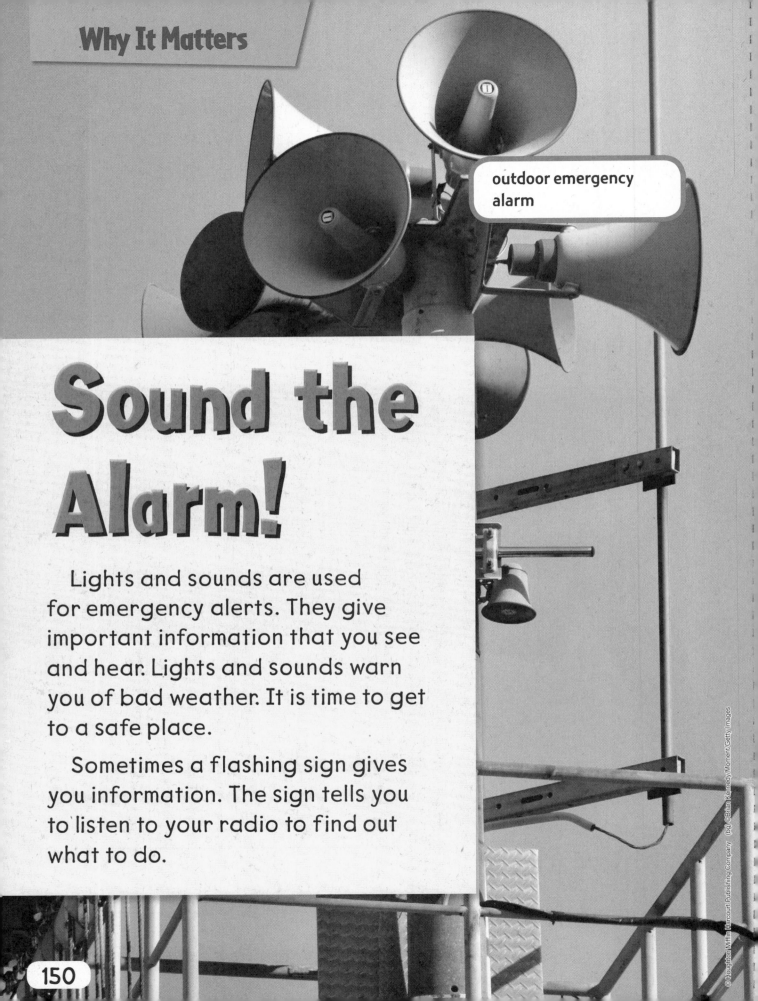

outdoor emergency alarm

Sound the Alarm!

Lights and sounds are used for emergency alerts. They give important information that you see and hear. Lights and sounds warn you of bad weather. It is time to get to a safe place.

Sometimes a flashing sign gives you information. The sign tells you to listen to your radio to find out what to do.

WINTER CONDITIONS DRIVE WITH CARE

► Circle pictures that show a sound alert. Draw an X on pictures that show a light alert.

POLICE

Sum It Up!

① Mark It!

Draw an X on an alert that uses light.
Circle an alert that uses sound.

② Draw It!

Draw two emergency signals that use light and sound.

light	sound

Brain Check

Name _____

Word Play

Unscramble the word to complete each sentence.

alert	evacuate	tornado	emergency

1. nmegereyc

   An ___ ___ ___ ___ ___ ___ ___ ___ ___ is a situation that needs immediate action.

2. rooatnd

   A ___ ___ ___ ___ ___ ___ ___ is a severe kind of weather.

3. vcueaeta

   You must ___ ___ ___ ___ ___ ___ ___ ___ a building if there is a fire.

4. telar

   A siren is an ___ ___ ___ ___ ___ or warning.

Apply Concepts

1. Use what you know about sound and light. Design an emergency alert. Show how it communicates over a distance.

Answer the question below.

2. How does your alert work? Write how it helps people in an emergency.

_____

_____

_____

_____

Take It Home!

Family Members: When you are walking or driving in your community, talk with your child about any emergency sounds and lights you hear and see. Discuss why each one is happening and how it keeps people safe.

Ask a Piano Tuner

Q. What is a piano tuner?

A. A piano tuner tunes pianos. A piano is *in tune* when its notes are all in the correct pitch.

Q. How do you tune a piano?

A. A string vibrates and makes a sound when you strike a key. The pitch changes when you tighten or loosen a string.

Q. What do you like best about your job?

A. I work in many places. I go to people's homes. I fix pianos in big concert halls, too.

Now It's Your Turn!

▶ What question would you ask a piano tuner?

_____

_____

_____

_____

Careers in Science continued

Out of Tune!

1 How does a piano make sound?

_____

_____

_____

2 What does it mean when a piano is _in tune_?

_____

_____

_____

3 How do you change a sound's pitch?

_____

_____

_____

Unit 4 Review

Name _____

Vocabulary Review

Use the terms in the box to complete the sentences.

energy
light
sound

1. An energy that you can hear is called _____.

2. Something that can do work and cause change has _____.

3. The energy that helps us see is called _____.

Science Concepts

Fill in the letter of the choice that best answers the question.

4. What is something that makes its own light?
   Ⓐ an electric lamp
   Ⓑ a flashlight
   Ⓒ the sun

5. Which object makes a sound that warns of a fire?
   Ⓐ someone saying hello
   Ⓑ a smoke detector
   Ⓒ a bike's bell

6. What is something that is needed in order to see objects clearly?

Ⓐ sound

Ⓑ light

Ⓒ pitch

7. Which object gives off heat and light?

Ⓐ energy

Ⓑ a police whistle

Ⓒ a campfire

8. Why do we need light?

Ⓐ to help us see in the dark

Ⓑ to help us sleep at night

Ⓒ to help us hear different pitches

9. How is sound made on this instrument?

Ⓐ The handle vibrates.

Ⓑ The strings vibrate.

Ⓒ The wood vibrates.

10. What is something a driver uses to see objects clearly at night?

Ⓐ a flashlight
Ⓑ headlights
Ⓒ the sun

11. What happens when you hit the top of a drum?

Ⓐ It hums.
Ⓑ It lights up.
Ⓒ It vibrates.

12. Which object gives off light?

 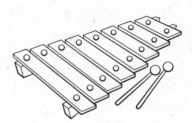

13. What happens to a shadow when an object moves closer to a light source?

Ⓐ It gets bigger.
Ⓑ It gets smaller.
Ⓒ It stays the same.

Inquiry and the Big Idea
Write the answers to these questions.

14. You want to read a book at night before bedtime.

   a. What tool can help you see it better?

   _____

   b. How does this tool help you?

   _____

   _____

15. Compare and contrast sound and light.

   a. How are they similar?

   _____

   _____

   b. Name a way they are different.

   _____

   _____

© Houghton Mifflin Harcourt Publishing Company

UNIT 5
Magnets

Big Idea

Magnets are used in everyday life. They attract some objects and repel others.

S1P2., S1P2.a, S1P2.b

I Wonder Why

A magnet does not attract a ball. Why?
Turn the page to find out.

Here's Why Magnets attract things made of iron or steel. A ball is made of plastic or rubber.

In this unit, you will explore this Big Idea, the Essential Questions, and the Investigations on the Inquiry Flipchart.

Levels of Inquiry Key ■ DIRECTED ■ GUIDED ■ INDEPENDENT

Track Your Progress

Big Idea Magnets are used in everyday life. They attract some objects and repel others.

Essential Questions

Lesson 1 How Do Magnets Move Objects? 163
  Inquiry Flipchart p. 21—Push and Pull/Which Magnet Will Win?
  S1P2.a; S1P2.b

Lesson 2 What Do Magnets Do? 173
  Inquiry Flipchart p. 22—What Do Magnets Do?
  S1P2.b

Careers in Science: Maglev Train Scientists 175

S.T.E.M. **Engineering and Technology:**
    Magnets All Around 177
  Inquiry Flipchart p. 23—Design It: Use Magnets
    S1P2.a

Unit 5 Review 179

Now I Get the Big Idea!

N | S

Science Notebook

Before you begin each lesson, be sure to write your thoughts about the Essential Question.

Essential Question

How Do Magnets Move Objects?

🧠 Engage Your Brain!

Find the answer to the question in the lesson.

What does a magnet do to iron and steel objects?

It _____ them.

Active Reading

Lesson Vocabulary

❶ Preview the lesson.

❷ Write the four vocabulary terms here.

_____   _____

_____   _____

It's Magnetic

What is pulling the paper clips? It is a magnet. A **magnet** pulls iron or steel objects. It can push or pull other magnets, too. Magnets can have different strengths.

Active Reading

A detail is a fact about a main idea. Draw one line under a detail. Draw an arrow to the main idea it tells about.

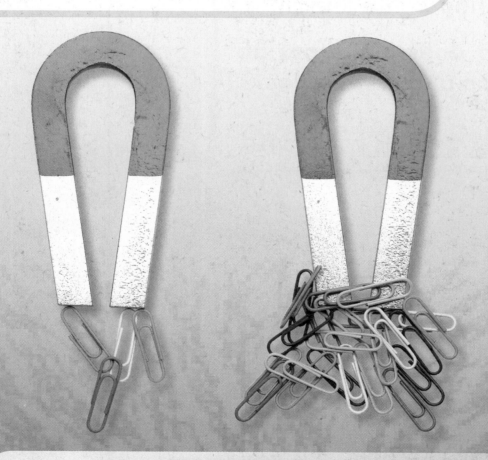

The magnet on the right is stronger. It pulls more than the other magnet.

Magnets have two poles. **Poles** are where the pull is the strongest. A magnet has an **N** pole and an **S** pole.

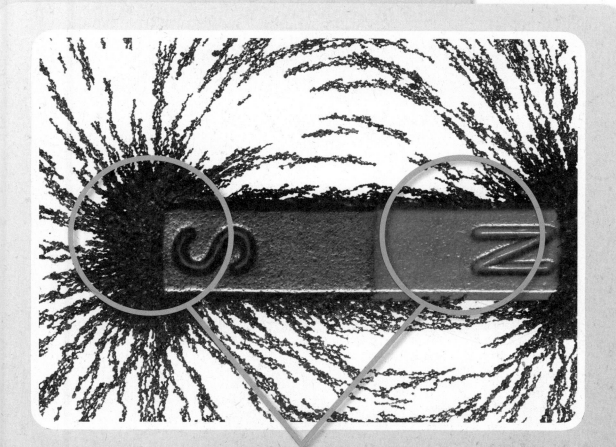

poles

▶ **Look at the magnet. Where is the pull the strongest?**

_____

_____

Get Together

A magnet can attract things. **Attract** means to pull something. A magnet pulls things made of iron or steel. It can pull things without touching them.

Opposite poles attract each other. The north and south poles attract.

N S

▶ Circle objects that a magnet attracts.

not attracting   attracting

Go Away!

A magnet does not always pull. Two magnets may repel. **Repel** means to push away. Like poles repel.

The two N poles and the two S poles repel each other.

MAGNETS ARE A MUST!

Did you know that you use magnets every day? Magnets are very useful. They help you in different ways. Look at each picture to find out why!

Electric can openers have magnets. The magnet holds the lid in place.

Pocketbooks use magnets. Some notebooks do, too! Magnets keep these objects closed.

▶ **Underline the reasons why these objects use magnets.**

Some doorbells use a magnet. The magnet helps make a buzzing or ringing sound.

▶ Write what might happen if a doorbell did not have a magnet.

_____

_____

A train set uses magnets. The magnets connect each of the railcars.

▶ Draw a picture. Show what you play with or use that has a magnet. Tell about it.

Sum It Up!

① Circle It!

Predict which object a magnet will attract. Circle it.

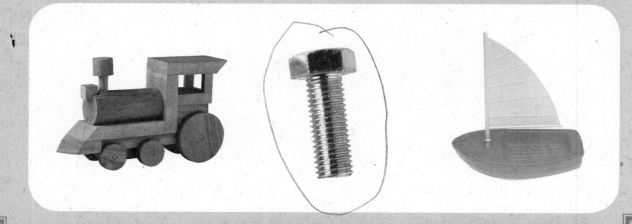

② Write It!

Think about objects you use that have magnets. Think about a way you might use a magnet, too. Write about it.

A toaster.

 **Brain Check**

Name _____

Word Play

Read each statement. Write your answer on the line below.

1 Describe what a magnet does when it attracts.

Stick together.

2 Describe what a magnet does when it repels.

Push apart

3 Describe the poles of a magnet.

one N one S.

Apply Concepts

Write the word that goes with each set of clues.

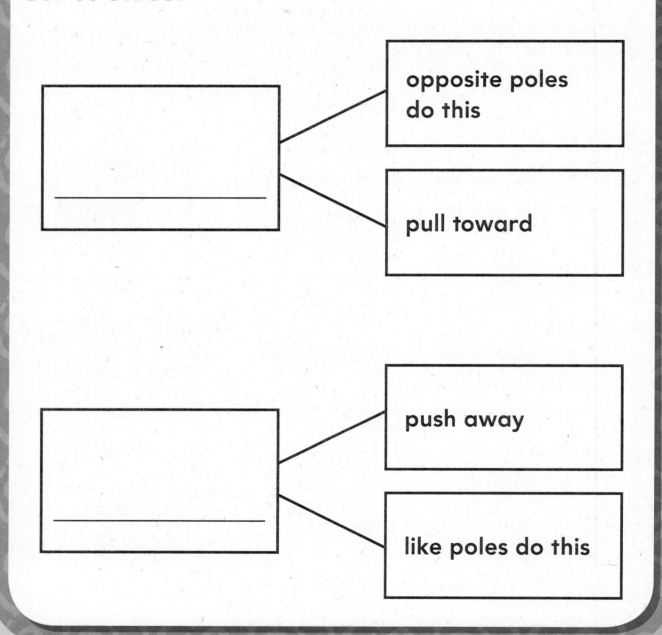

```
[                    ]  ──  opposite poles
[                    ]      do this
[ _____   ]
[                    ]  ──  pull toward
```

```
[                    ]  ──  push away
[                    ]
[ _____   ]
[                    ]  ──  like poles do this
```

Take It Home!

Family Members: Ask your child to tell you about magnets. Encourage them to tell you how they work. Ask them to tell how magnets are used in everyday life.

Inquiry Flipchart p. 22

Name _____

Essential Question
What Do Magnets Do?

Set a Purpose
Write what you want to find out.

_____

_____

State Your Hypothesis
Write your hypothesis, or the statement that you will test.

_____

_____

Think About the Procedure
Why is it important to test what a magnet attracts with different classroom objects and other magnets?

_____

_____

Record Your Data

Record your observations in this chart. Write the names of the four objects you tested. Circle **attracts** or **does not attract** based on your results.

Object	Attracts/Does Not Attract	
	attracts	does not attract
	attracts	does not attract
	attracts	does not attract
	attracts	does not attract

Draw Conclusions

1 What happens when like poles are pushed together? What happens when opposite poles are pushed together? Which objects does a magnet attract?

_____

2 Why do you think that happens?

_____

Ask More Questions

What other questions can you ask about magnets?

_____

Ask a Scientist About Maglev Trains

What is a maglev train?

A maglev train uses magnets to lift and move it forward. The train goes very, very fast. It takes a lot less time to get from place to place on this kind of train. The ride is smooth and not bumpy!

What does a scientist do?

I conduct research. I make sure a maglev train uses less energy to power it than other trains. I build trains that are quiet. I want to find ways to reduce the cost of the train track.

What is one problem that scientists are working on?

Today, some maglev trains travel more than 300 miles per hour. I am designing a train that will go much faster. I will test the train so it is safe to travel in.

Now It's Your Turn!

▶ What question would you ask?

_____

_____

_____

_____

Design Your Own Maglev Train

▶ Draw your own maglev train.

▶ Write about what moves your maglev train. Tell about what it is like to ride in it.

_____

_____

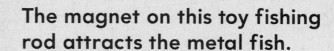

Magnets All Around

Everyday Magnets

Magnets are used in many things we use.

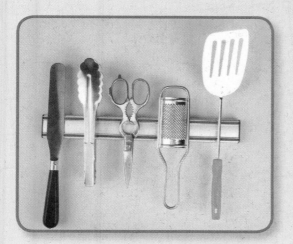

A magnet keeps these kitchen tools in place.

The magnet on this toy fishing rod attracts the metal fish.

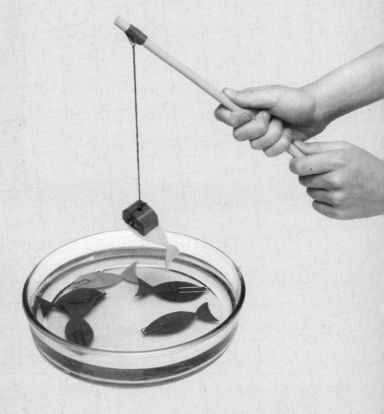

Magnets help keep the refrigerator door closed. Then the food inside stays cold.

S.T.E.M.
continued

Magnets I Use

Draw two ways that you use magnets every day.

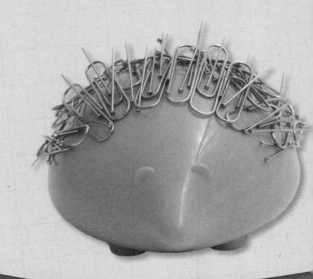

What are the ways you use magnets every day? Write about it.

_____

_____

Build On It!

Find your own way to use magnets. Complete **Design It: Use Magnets** on the Inquiry Flipchart.

Name _____

Vocabulary Review

Use the terms in the box to complete the sentences.

> Attract
> magnet
> poles

1. Something that pulls iron or steel objects is called a _____.

2. Magnets have two _____.

3. _____ means to pull something.

Science Concepts

Fill in the letter of the choice that best answers the question.

4. Two N poles will
   Ⓐ attract each other.
   Ⓑ repel each other.
   Ⓒ push and pull.

5. The N pole and the S pole will
   Ⓐ push and pull.
   Ⓑ repel each other.
   Ⓒ attract each other.

6. What kind of objects does a magnet attract?
   (A) objects made from iron or steel
   (B) all objects
   (C) only other magnets

7. What does this picture show?

   (A) Magnets must touch objects to attract them.
   (B) Magnets can attract objects without touching them.
   (C) Magnets must touch objects to repel them.

8. Which word tells what happens when two magnets pull toward each other?
   (A) pole
   (B) repel
   (C) attract

9. Which of these objects will a magnet attract? Predict it.
   (A)
   (B)
   (C)

10. What everyday object does not use a magnet?
  Ⓐ a plate
  Ⓑ a pocketbook
  Ⓒ a doorbell

11. Why does a refrigerator have magnets inside of it?

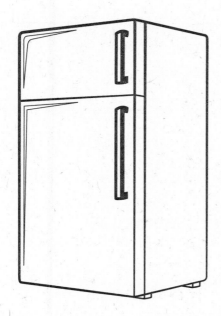

  Ⓐ to keep the door shut so food stays cold
  Ⓑ to let air in so the food does not spoil
  Ⓒ to make opening the door much easier

12. What does a magnet do on this electric can opener?

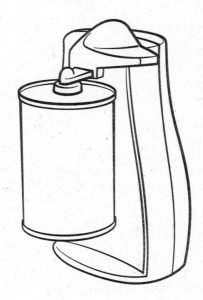

  Ⓐ It opens the can.
  Ⓑ It keeps the lid from falling into the can.
  Ⓒ It keeps the can strong.

Inquiry and the Big Idea
Write the answers to these questions.

13. Compare the magnets. Describe what they are doing. How do you know?

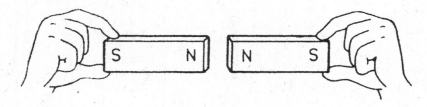

_____

_____

14. Look at this object.

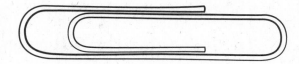

a. How could you move the object without touching it?

_____

b. Why can you move the object that way?

_____

_____

UNIT 6
Living Things

Big Idea

Plants have parts to help them meet their basic needs. Animals meet their basic needs, too. Their needs are similar and different.

S1L1, S1L1.a, S1L1.b, S1L1.c

I Wonder Why

Plants and animals need air, water, and space. Why?
Turn the page to find out.

Here's Why Plants and animals need air, water, and space in order to live and grow in a healthy way.

In this unit, you will explore this Big Idea, the Essential Questions, and the Investigations on the Inquiry Flipchart.

Levels of Inquiry Key ■ DIRECTED ■ GUIDED ■ INDEPENDENT

Track Your Progress

Big Idea Plants have parts to help them meet their basic needs. Animals meet their basic needs, too. Their needs are similar and different.

Essential Questions

Lesson 1 **What Do Plants Need?** 185
> Inquiry Flipchart p. 24—Grow to the Light/Colored Celery
> S1L1.b

Inquiry Lesson 2 **Why Do Plants Grow?** 195
> Inquiry Flipchart p. 25—Why Do Plants Grow?
> S1L1.b

Lesson 3 **What Are Some Parts of Plants?** 197
> Inquiry Flipchart p. 26—Are All Seeds Alike?/What Parts Do You See?
> S1L1.a

Lesson 4 **What Do Animals Need?** 207
> Inquiry Flipchart p. 27—Meet the Mealworm/Eat Like a Bird
> S1L1.b

Careers in Science: Ask a Zookeeper 219
> S1L1.c

S.T.E.M. **Engineering and Technology: Tool Time** 221
> Inquiry Flipchart p. 28—Design It: A New Tool

Unit 6 Review 223

Now I Get the Big Idea!

Science Notebook

Before you begin each lesson, be sure to write your thoughts about the Essential Question.

Essential Question

What Do Plants Need?

Engage Your Brain!

Find the answer to the question in the lesson.

How does this plant grow without soil?

Its roots take in

_____

_____.

Active Reading

Lesson Vocabulary

1 Preview the lesson.

2 Write the three vocabulary terms here.

_____   _____

_____

Plant Needs

Sunlight, Air, and Water

A plant needs certain things to live and grow. A plant needs **sunlight**, or light from the sun. It also needs air and water. A plant uses these things to make its food.

Active Reading

The main idea is the most important idea about something. Draw two lines under the main idea.

Air is all around us, even though we can not see it.

Plants grow toward the sun to get the light they need.

Plants get most of the water they need from the soil.

▶ **Circle three words that name things a plant needs.**

From the Soil

Most plants need soil to grow. **Soil** is made up of small pieces of rock and once-living things. A plant's roots take in water from the soil. The roots take in nutrients, too. **Nutrients** are things in soil that help plants grow.

Some plants do not grow in soil. They live and grow on other plants. Their roots take in rain and water from the air.

A detail is a fact about a main idea. Draw one line under a detail. Draw an arrow to the main idea it tells about.

Space to Grow

As a plant grows, its stem gets taller. Its roots get bigger. It grows more leaves, too. A plant must have enough space to grow.

▶ **What does this farmer do to make sure that his crop grows?**

_____

_____

_____

People Helping Plants

How do people help plants? They water plants. They pull weeds so plants have space to grow. People put plants by windows so the plants can get sunlight.

Active Reading

Clue words can help you find an effect. **So** is a clue word. Draw a box around **so**.

People also help plants by planting new ones. They plant seeds so new flowers can grow. They plant young trees so people can enjoy them.

▶ **How do you help plants?**

_____

_____

Sum It Up!

1 Circle It!

Circle two things that a plant needs.

2 Write It!

This plant has gotten too big for its pot.

What need is not being met?

_____

Brain Check

Name _____

Word Play

Write each word next to the part of the picture it tells about.

| water | sunlight | soil | air |

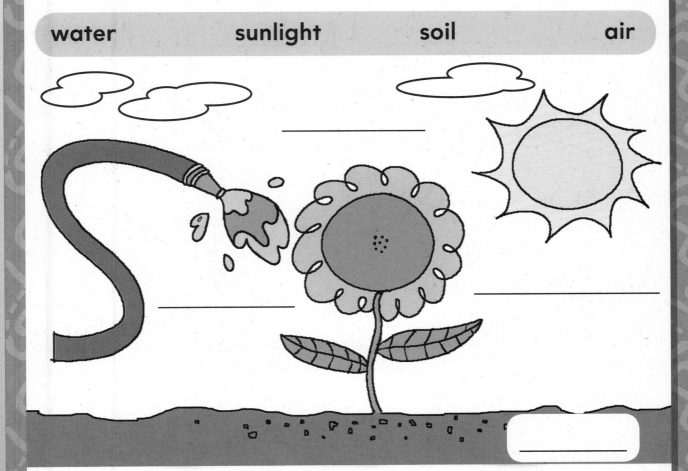

Answer the question.

What things in soil help plants grow?

_____

Apply Concepts

Complete the web to tell what plants need to grow and be healthy.

Plant Needs

Family Members: See *ScienceSaurus*® for more information about plants.

Name _____

Essential Question
Why Do Plants Grow?

Set a Purpose

Tell what you want to find out.

_____

_____

Think About the Procedure

❶ What will you observe?

_____

_____

❷ How will you treat the plants differently?

_____

_____

Record Your Data

In this chart, record what you observe.

My Observations of Two Plants		
	Plant A	**Plant B**
How the stems look		
How the leaves look		
Other observations		

Draw Conclusions

Can a plant grow when it does not get what it needs?

_____

_____

Ask More Questions

What other questions could you ask about plant needs?

_____

_____

Essential Question

What Are Some Parts of Plants?

Engage Your Brain!

Find the answer to the question in the lesson.

What holds this tree in place?

its _____

Active Reading

Lesson Vocabulary

① Preview the lesson.

② Write the six vocabulary terms here.

_____ _____

_____ _____

_____ _____

A Plant's Makeup

A plant has parts that help it grow and change.

Taking Root

A plant has roots that grow into the soil. The **roots** hold the plant in place. They take in water from the soil. They take in other things from the soil that the plant needs.

roots

© Houghton Mifflin Harcourt Publishing Company (bl) ©Theo Allofs/Getty Images

Stems Stand Tall

The **stem** holds up the plant. It takes water from the roots to the other parts of the plant.

A flower has a thin, soft stem. A tree has a thick, woody stem, called a trunk.

stems

▶ Draw a triangle around the roots of the bean plant. Draw a circle around the stem.

Leaves at Work

A **leaf** is a plant part that makes food for the plant. It uses light, air, and water.

Active Reading

Find the sentence that tells the meaning of **leaf**. Draw a line under the sentence.

Leaves can be different shapes and sizes.

banana leaf

pine needles

clover

ash

red maple

Flowers, Seeds, and Fruit

Many plants have flowers. A **flower** is a plant part that makes seeds. A new plant may grow from a **seed**. The new plant will look like the plant that made the seed.

Many flowers grow into fruits. A **fruit** holds seeds.

fruit

flowers

seeds

▶ Draw a circle around the leaves. Draw an X on the flowers and fruits.

Plant Power

We use plants for food. We also use plants to make things. Mint leaves are used in some toothpastes. Flowers make perfume smell good. Woody stems help make our homes. We even use plants to make some medicines. What other plant uses can you name?

Do the Math!
Solve a Problem

Look at the tomatoes. Use them to help you solve this problem.

A farmer has 24 tomatoes.
He picks 11 tomatoes.
How many are left?

_____ - _____ = _____

Sum It Up!

① Choose It!

Circle the plant part that takes in water.

② Solve It!

Solve each riddle.

I can be thick or thin.
I can be short or tall.
I help a plant get
water and hold it up so
it won't fall.

What am I?

_____

I can be different colors,
shapes, and sizes.
I may fall to the ground.
I take in light and air to
make food for a plant
since it can't move around.

What am I?

_____

204

 Brain Check

Name _____

Word Play

Label the parts of the plant.

| flower | leaf | roots | stem |

_____

_____

_____

_____

Apply Concepts

Tell which plant parts the plant needs.

Problem	Solution
❶ I need a plant part to hold seeds. What part do I need?	_____
❷ I need a plant part to take in water. What part do I need?	_____
❸ I need a plant part to make fruit. What part do I need?	_____
❹ I need a plant part to make food. What part do I need?	_____
❺ I need a plant part to hold me up. What part do I need?	_____
❻ I need a plant part to make a plant just like me. What part do I need?	_____

Take It Home!

Family Members: Encourage your child to tell you about the parts of the plant. Then have your child ask you questions to identify plant parts.

Essential Question

What Do Animals Need?

Engage Your Brain!

Find the answer to the question in the lesson.

Why is a clownfish shelter unusual?

A clownfish lives

_____.

Active Reading

Lesson Vocabulary

1 Preview the lesson.

2 Write the two vocabulary terms here.

_____ _____

Animal Needs

Food and Water

Animals need food and water to grow and stay healthy. Some animals eat plants. Some eat other animals. Still others eat both plants and animals.

Active Reading

The main idea is the most important idea about something. Draw two lines under the main idea.

A deer drinks water.

Air

Almost all animals need oxygen, a gas in air. Land animals use their lungs to breathe in oxygen.

Some water animals, like whales, have lungs. They breathe air. Fish do not have lungs. They use **gills** to get oxygen.

A black bear uses its lungs to breathe.

gills

A fish uses gills to take in oxygen from the water.

▶ **Which animal uses its gills to get oxygen?**

_____

Shelter

Most animals need shelter. A **shelter** is a place where an animal can be safe. An animal may use a plant as a shelter. It may dig a hole in the ground. It may even use another animal as a shelter. One animal that does this is a clownfish.

Kinds of Animal Shelters

A prairie dog lives in a burrow.

A beaver lives in a lodge.

Some birds lay eggs in a nest.

A skunk lives in a den.

▶ Draw an animal in its shelter.

Space

Animals need space to grow. They need space to move around and find food.

Animals need space for shelter. They need space to take care of their young.

A detail is a fact about a main idea. Draw one line under a detail. Draw an arrow to the main idea it tells about.

A cheetah needs space to run and catch its food.

© Houghton Mifflin Harcourt Publishing Company (bkgd) ©Andrew Harrington/Alamy

Comparing Animals and Plants

Animals and plants have some of the same needs. They have different needs, too. Look at the chart to see how they are alike and different.

Animals	Plants
air	light
water	water
food	air
shelter	nutrients
space to grow	space to grow

▶ Circle words in each column that tell how the needs of animals and plants are alike.

▶ Write questions that compare and contrast the needs of the bird and grapevine pictured on the page.

_____

_____

Caring for Pets

Pets are animals. Think about some pets you know. Where do they get their food and water? Who gives them shelter? They need people to help them meet their needs.

Taking care of a pet is a big job. A pet needs space to exercise and play. You need to keep the pet and its shelter clean. You must clean up after a pet, too.

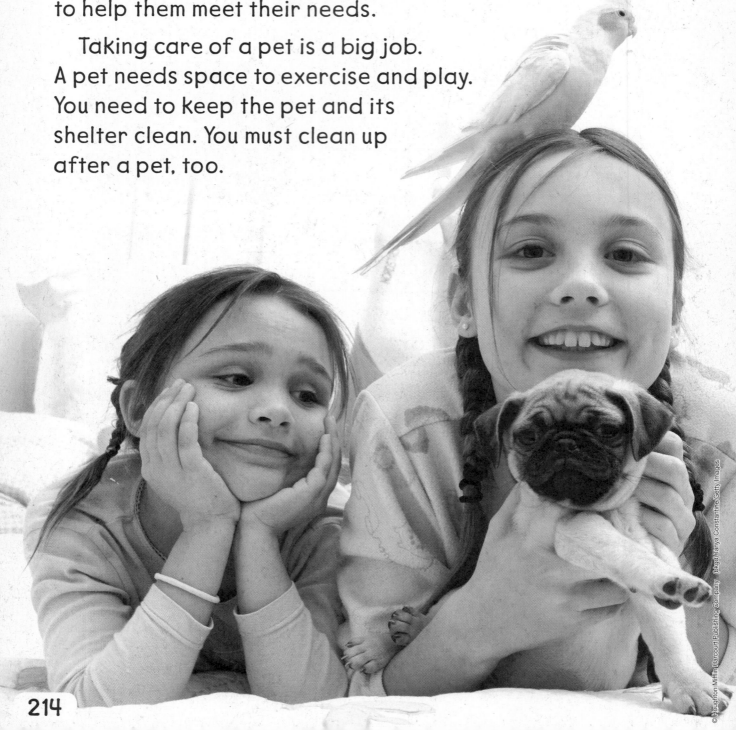

People need to take care of pets and keep them clean.

People need to give pets food.

This dog gets 1 cup of dog food in the morning and 1 cup of dog food at night.

How many cups of dog food does it get for 1 day?

1 cup in morning
+ 1 cup at night
_____

_____ cups in one day

How many cups of dog food does it get for 5 days?

_____

Sum It Up!

① Choose It!

Mark an X on the need that does <u>not</u> belong.

Animal Needs

water   sunlight

air   food

② Circle It!

How are animals and plants alike?

They both need soil.

They both need nutrients.

They both need sunlight and nutrients.

They both need water, air, and space to grow.

③ Draw It!

Draw the animal you might find in each shelter.

nest	burrow

Name _____

Word Play

Pets need things to help them live and grow.
Fill in the words to tell what a hamster needs.

air   food   shelter   space to grow   water

a_____

w_____

s_____

s_____   f_____

217

Apply Concepts

You read about how animals and plants have needs. Now think about how you meet your needs each day. Fill in the chart below.

You Need	How You Meet Your Needs
1 air	_____ _____
2 _____	I drink from the water fountain at soccer practice.
3 food	_____ _____
4 _____	I go inside my house when it rains.
5 space to grow	_____ _____

Take It Home!

Family Members: Discuss with your child what animals and people need to grow and stay healthy. Ask your child to tell you how his or her needs are met.

Ask a Zoo Keeper

What does a zoo keeper do?

I feed the animals. I give them water. I make sure that the animals are healthy. I also keep their environments clean.

How do you know when an animal is sick?

Animals can not tell me when they don't feel well. So I observe them carefully. Sometimes an animal eats or moves very little. That could be a sign that the animal is sick.

What else does a zoo keeper do?

I talk to people about the zoo animals. I have fun talking to children. They like animals so much!

Now It's Your Turn!

▶ **What question would you ask a zoo keeper?**

_____

_____

Now You Be a Zoo Keeper!

▶ A tiger cub was born at your zoo. Make a plan to take care of the cub.

My Zoo Keeper Plan

1 I will _____
   _____.

2 I will _____
   _____.

3 I will _____
   _____.

Tool Time

How We Use Tools

Some animals dig holes and use plants for shelter. Other animals use shelters that are built by other animals. People need shelters, too. They use tools to build them. Tool are objects that people use to make a job easier.

One kind of shelter that people build is a house. They use many tools to build it.

drill

hammer

The Best Tool for the Job

Draw a line to match each tool to how it is used.

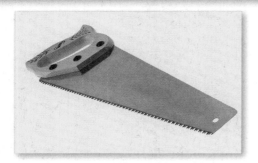

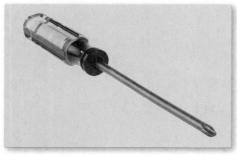

Build On It!

You can design your own tool. Complete **Design It: A New Tool** on the Inquiry Flipchart.

Unit 6 Review

Vocabulary Review

Use the terms in the box to complete the sentences.

> nutrients
> roots
> shelter

1. Two things from soil that help a plant grow are water and _____.

2. A plant is held in place by its _____.

3. Animals dig holes and use other animals as _____.

Science Concepts

Fill in the letter of the choice that best answers the question.

4. How are all animals the same?
   Ⓐ All animals need food and water.
   Ⓑ All animals live in the same place.
   Ⓒ All animals move in the same way.

5. How could you find out if plants need light to live?
   Ⓐ Grow two plants. Give both plants water.
   Ⓑ Grow two plants. Give only one plant light.
   Ⓒ Grow two plants. Give only one plant water.

6. What do animals and plants both need to live and grow?

  Ⓐ food, water, and shelter

  Ⓑ nutrients and sunlight

  Ⓒ air, water, space to grow

7. Which of these plant parts is a kind of stem?

  Ⓐ apple

  Ⓑ tree trunk

  Ⓒ pine needle

8. A plant needs more space to grow. Which would give the plant more space?

  Ⓐ giving it more water

  Ⓑ putting more plants around it

  Ⓒ pulling up weeds around it

9. Which plant part does Number 3 show?

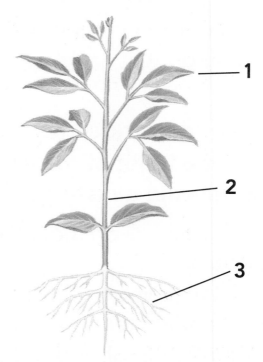

  Ⓐ leaf

  Ⓑ stem

  Ⓒ roots

10. How are plants **different** from animals?

Ⓐ Plants need water and air.

Ⓑ Plants need space to grow.

Ⓒ Plants make their own food.

11. Which is true about an animal you keep as a pet?

Ⓐ It does not have basic needs.

Ⓑ It needs people to help it meet its needs.

Ⓒ It does not need shelter or food.

12. Read these steps for how a plant gets and uses water.

1. The roots take in water from the soil.

2. _____?

3. The leaves use water to make food.

Which step is missing?

Ⓐ The plant grows taller.

Ⓑ The flowers grow into fruit.

Ⓒ Water moves through the stem to all of the leaves.

Inquiry and the Big Idea
Write the answers to these questions.

13. Look at this deer.

   a. What need is the deer meeting?

   _____

   b. Name two other needs the deer has.

   _____

   c. What happens to the deer if its basic needs are
      not met?

   _____

14. Look at this picture.

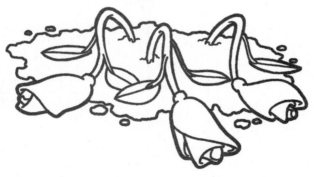

   a. How do you know that the plant is not meeting its
      basic needs?

   _____

   b. Name two things the plant needs.

   _____

Technology and Coding

Have you ever wondered how video games are made? Or how a cell phone works? If so, you might like computer science! Computer science is the study of computer technology.

What Computers Can Do

Computers are machines that take in, manage, and store information. You can solve math problems with a computer. You can make art or music with a computer. Computers can do many things.

Do you recognize these objects? They use computer technology.

Computers are all around you. Even some toasters and cars use computer technology!

_____

_____

_____

_____

Draw another example here.

_____

Let's Talk!

How do computers help solve problems? They follow instructions, or programs, that people make.

Programs are written in a special language, or code. Computers understand the code and follow its instructions. If you learn the code, you can write computer programs, too!

```
dog.speed = 5;
play_sound(woof);
```

People who work in computer science have many skills. They are creative and like to solve problems.

Designing and writing a computer program is like solving a puzzle. The computer follows the program's instructions exactly and in order. If something is missing, the program won't work as planned.

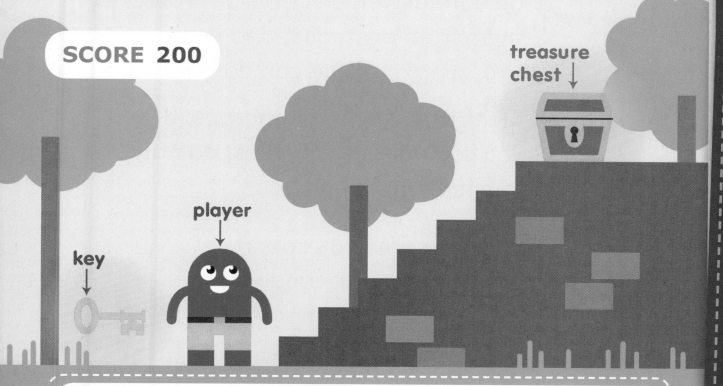

SCORE 200

treasure chest ↓

player ↓

key ↓

How would you move the player to the treasure chest? Explain the steps.

_____

_____

_____

Play it Safe

- ✓ Be careful with electronics. Protect them from dust, dirt, and water. Dropping a device can damage it.

- ✓ Electricity can be dangerous. If you see damaged cables, do not touch them. Tell an adult.

- ✓ Limit the time you spend on electronics. Take breaks to exercise or stretch.

- ✓ Talk to your family about rules for the Internet. Do not share private information on your computer or phone. This includes pictures and passwords.

Circle the pictures that show how to use electronics safely. Place an X over the pictures that do not.

Careers in Computing

Do you like art and working with computers? If so, you might enjoy a career in computer animation!

Animators make characters for movies and video games. They use computer programs to design a character and make its body move.

Interactive Glossary

This Interactive Glossary will help you learn how to spell a vocabulary term. The glossary will give you the meaning of the term. It will also show you a picture to help you understand what the term means.

Where you see **Your Turn** write your own words or draw your own picture to help you remember what the term means.

A

alert
A warning. (p. 148)

Your Turn

attract
To pull something. (p. 166)

D

design process
A plan with steps that helps engineers find good solutions. (p. 49)

Interactive Glossary

E

energy
Something that can do work and cause change. (p. 124)

evacuate
To leave. (p. 148)

Your Turn →

engineer
Someone who uses math and science to solve problems. (p. 48)

F

flower
The part of a plant that makes seeds. (p. 201)

fruit

The part of the plant that holds seeds. (p. 201)

Your Turn

H

human-made

Materials made by people. (p. 66)

G

gills

The parts of a fish that take in oxygen from the water. (p. 209)

gills →

I

inquiry skills

Skills that help you find out information. (p. 18)

Falling Leaves Forest

observe

compare

Interactive Glossary

investigation
A test that scientists do.
(p. 30)

light
Energy that lets you see.
(p. 124)

L

leaf
The part of a plant that makes food for the plant. A leaf uses light, air, and water to make food. (p. 200)

Your Turn

loudness
How loud or soft a sound is.
(p. 136)

M

magnet
Something that pulls iron or steel objects. (p. 164)

materials
What objects are made of. (p. 64)

N

natural
Materials found in nature. (p. 66)

Interactive Glossary

nutrients
Things in soil that help plants grow. (p. 188)

poles
Where the pull is the strongest on a magnet. (p. 165)

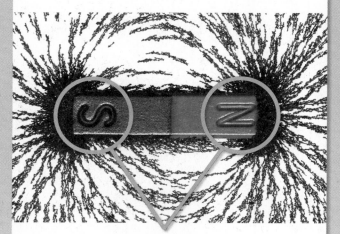

poles

Your Turn

P

pitch
How high or low a sound is. (p. 137)

R

precipitation
Liquid or solid water that falls from the clouds toward the ground. (p. 88)

Your Turn

repel
To push away. (p. 167)

roots
The part of a plant that holds the plant in place. The roots take in water and nutrients. (p. 198)

Interactive Glossary

S

science tools
Tools people use to find out about things. (p. 8)

seed
The part of a plant that new plants grow from. (p. 201)

season
A time of year that has a certain kind of weather. The four seasons are spring, summer, fall, and winter. (p. 104)

Your Turn

senses
The way you observe and learn. The five senses are sight, hearing, smell, taste, and touch. (p. 4)

shelter

A place where an animal can be safe. (p. 210)

sound

Energy you can hear. (p. 134)

Your Turn →

soil

The top layer of Earth. It is made up of small pieces of rock and once-living things. (p. 188)

Interactive Glossary

stem

The part of a plant that holds up the plant. (p. 199)

Your Turn

sunlight

Light that comes from the sun. (p. 186)

T

temperature

A measure of how hot or cold something is. (p. 86)

tornado

A very strong wind that comes down from clouds in the shape of a funnel. (p. 149)

V

vibrate

To move quickly back and forth. (p. 135)

W

weather

What the air outside is like. (p. 84)

Interactive Glossary

weather pattern
A change in the weather that repeats. (p. 104)

wind
Air that moves. (p. 84)

Your Turn

Index

A

Active Reading, 3, 4, 8, 17, 18, 29, 30, 32, 34, 47, 48, 52, 61, 62, 64, 68, 83, 84, 86, 90, 103, 104, 108, 123, 124, 125, 133, 134, 136, 147, 148, 163, 164, 167, 185, 186, 188, 190, 197, 198, 200, 207, 208, 212. *See also* **Reading Skills**

air
  for animals, 209
  for plants, 186, 200
alert, 138, 147–151, R1
Anderson, Mary, 39–40
animals. *See also* **birds; fish and ocean animals; insect**
  basic needs, 183–184, 207–212, 213, 219–220, 221
  beaver, 210
  birds, 105
  black bear, 209
  cheetah, 212
  deer, 208
  dinosaurs, 1–2
  dog, 138, 139, 215
  in fall, 108, 109
  growth of, 208
  hare, 107, 111
  pet care, 214–215
  plants and, 213
  prairie dog, 210
  seasonal changes and, 105–111
  skunk, 211
  in spring, 105
  squirrel, 109
  in summer, 106, 107
  tiger, 220
  in winter, 110, 111
  in zoo, 219–220
animator, 234
architect, 75–76
Ask More Questions, 16, 28, 60, 74, 98, 132, 144, 174, 196
attract, 161, 166, 173–174, R1

B

Bacon-Bercey, June, 101
balance, 9
bicycles, 62–63
birds
  bones, 75
  graph, 20
  in spring, 105
  needs of, 213
  nests, 211
breathing, 209
brick, 64, 65
building, in design process, 52–53

C

campfires, 125
Careers in Computing, 234

Careers in Science
  animator, 234
  computer science, 231
  maglev train design, 175–176
  piano tuner, 155–156
  zoo keeper, 219–220
cars
  headlights, 126
  windshield wipers, 39–40
cell phone, 149
Children's Museum, Indianapolis, 1
children's playground, 45
civil engineer, 49
classify, 20
clouds
  hailstones, 91
  precipitation, 88
clue words, 30, 52, 190
coding, 227–231
colors
  mixing, 29, 30–35
  seeing, 7
communicating, 20, 55
compare, 18
  plants and animals, 213
computer, 227–231
computer animation, 23
computer programming, 230–231
computer science, 227, 230–231

Index

computer technology, 227–231
contrast, 136
  plants and animals, 213
cotton, 66–69
crops, 189

daylight
  in fall, 108
  in summer, 106
  in winter, 110
design process, 49–55, R1
  communicating, 55
  finding a problem, 50–51
  planning and building, 52–53
  redesigning, 55
  testing and improving, 54
doorbell, 169
Do the Math!
  compare numbers, 92
  measure length, 11
  solve a problem, 203, 215
Draw Conclusions, 16, 28, 60, 74, 98, 132, 144, 174, 196
drawing conclusions, 22, 33
drum, 135, 137

ears, 4
eggs, bird, 211
electric can openers, 168
electricity, light from, 126
electronics, 227–231
  safety, 232–233
emergency alerts, 138, 147–151
energy, 124, R2
  light, 121, 124
  sound, 121, 134
engineer, 45–46, 47–55, R2
  architect, 75–76
  civil, 49
  mechanical, 49
  as problem solver, 48–49
  robotics, 48
Engineering and Technology. *See also* **S.T.E.M. (Science, Technology, Engineering, and Mathematics)**
  coding, 227–231
  computers, 227–231, 234
  magnets, 177–178
  telephones, 145–146
  tools, 221–222
  weather tools, 115–116

engineering design process, 49–55
  communicating, 55
  finding a problem, 50–51
  planning and building, 52–53
  redesigning, 55
  testing and improving, 54
evacuate, 148, R2
eyes, 5

fall season, 108–109
finding a problem, in design process, 50–51
fire
  campfires, 125
  emergency alerts, 148
fish and ocean animals
  clownfish, 207, 210
  gills, 209
  lungs, 209
  scales, 75
flashlights, 125
flower, R2
  for perfume, 202
  in spring, 104
flowers, 199, 201
food
  for animals, 208, 212
  for pets, 214–215
  for plants, 186
  plants used for, 202–203
fruit, 106, 201, R3

G

gills, 209, R3
glass, 64, 65
graph, 20
growth
    of animals, 208
    of plants, 186–189,
        195–196
guitar, 135

H

hailstones, 91
hand lens, 8
hands, 5
headlamps, 125
hearing, 6
houses, 64–65
human-made material,
    66–67, R3
humans
    in fall, 108
    helping plants, 190–191
    materials made by,
        66–67
    senses of, 3–7
    shelter for, 221
    in spring, 104, 105
    in summer, 106
    in winter, 110
hypothesizing, 21, 31

I

ice, 81–82
    hailstones, 91
    sleet, 90

ice crystals, 89
ice pellets, 90
improving, in design
    process, 54
infer, 22
Inquiry Skills, 18, R3.
    See also **scientific
    inquiry**
    Ask More Questions,
        16, 28, 60, 74,
        98, 132, 144, 174,
        196
    Draw Conclusions, 16,
        28, 60, 74, 98, 132,
        144, 174, 196
    to help you learn,
        18–23
    Picture Cards, 99
    Record Data, 16, 28,
        60, 74, 98, 132, 144,
        174, 196
    Set a Purpose, 15, 27,
        59, 73, 97, 131, 143,
        173, 195
    State Your Hypothesis,
        173
    Think About the
        Procedure, 15, 27,
        59, 73, 97, 131, 143,
        173, 195
    using, 26–27
insect, dragonfly, 75
investigation, 30–35,
    R4
iron, magnets and,
    163, 164, 166

K

Kearns, Robert, 40

L

leaf, 200, R4
leaves, 189, 200
    ash, 200
    banana, 200
    clover, 200
    in fall, 108
    kinds of, 200
    pine needles, 200
    red maple, 200
    in spring, 105
    in summer, 107
    uses of, 202
    in winter, 103, 110
light, 121–122, 123–127,
    R4. *See also* **sunlight**
    campfires, 125
    from electricity, 126
    emergency alerts,
        147–151
    flashlights, 125
    headlamps, 125
    headlights, 126
    for plants, 186, 187,
        190, 200
    shadows and,
        131–132
    sources of, 124–125
    street lights, 126
    from the sun, 124
    uses of, 126–127,
        147–151

© Houghton Mifflin Harcourt Publishing Company

Index

living things, 183–184.
  See also **animals;
  people; plants**
  soil and, 188
loudness, 136–137, R4
lungs, of animals, 209

maglev trains, 175–176
magnet(s), 161–169, R5
  attracting objects, 161,
    166, 173–174
  everyday life uses,
    168–169, 177–178
  maglev trains, 175–176
  objects moved by,
    163–169
  poles, 165, 166, 167
  repelling objects, 161,
    167, 173–174
  strengths of, 164
  uses of, 173–174
Main Idea, 167, 186, 208
Main Idea and Details,
  4, 32, 34, 48, 62, 84, 90,
  108, 164, 188, 198, 212
materials, 61–69, R5
  everyday, 68–69
  human-made, 66–67
  natural, 66–67
  objects and, 62–65
  sorting, 73–74
measure, 10–11, 19
  rain, 87
  temperature, 86
  weather, 86–87

measuring cup, 9
measuring tools, 9
mechanical engineer, 49
medicine, 202
metal, 64, 65, 66
  magnets and, 163,
    164, 166, 177
meteorologist, 101
model, 23
mouth, 5
musical instruments,
  135, 137, 155–156

natural material,
  66–67, R5
nature, architectural
  forms from, 75–76
nose, 5
notebooks, 168
N pole, 165, 166, 167
nutrients, R6
  for plants, 188
  in soil, 188
nylon, 66, 67

objects, 62–65. *See also*
  materials
  moved by magnets,
    163–169
observe, 7, 18, 30
  weather, 92–93, 97–99
oxygen, for animals,
  209

patterns, weather,
  104, 105, 106, 108, 110
people
  in fall, 108
  helping plants, 190–191
  materials made by,
    66–67
  senses of, 3–7
  shelter for, 221
  in spring, 104, 105
  in summer, 106
  in winter, 110
People in Science
  Anderson, Mary, 39–40
  Bacon-Bercey, June,
    101
  Kearns, Robert, 40
  Tssui, Eugene, 75–76
petroleum, 66
pets, 214–215
piano tuner, 155–156
Picture Cards, 99
pine needles, 200
pitch, 137, R6
planning
  in design process,
    52–53
  investigations, 21, 31
plants. *See also* **flower;
  leaves; roots; seed(s);
  stem(s); trees**
  animals and, 213
  for animal shelter,
    221

basic needs, 183–184,
  185–189, 213
celery, 15–16
eaten by animals, 208
in fall, 108–109
grapevine, 213
growth of, 186–189,
  195–196
how people help,
  190–191
parts of, 197–201
seasonal changes and,
  104–111
in spring, 105
in summer, 106–107
tomato, 203
used as food, 202–203
uses of, 202–203
in winter, 110–111
plastic, 66, 67
pocketbooks, 168
poles, magnetic, 165,
  166, 167, R6
police cars, 121–122
precipitation, 88, R7
  forms of, 88–91
  hailstones, 91
  measuring, 87
  rain, 88
  sleet, 90
  snow, 89
predict, 19
  weather, 92–93
problem solving,
  48–49, 59–60, 203, 215
  with computers, 230,
  231

R

rain, 88
  measuring, 87
  sleet, 90
  in spring, 105
rain gauge, 87
Reading Skills, 3, 4, 8,
  17, 18, 29, 30, 32, 34,
  47, 48, 52, 61, 62, 64,
  68, 83, 84, 86, 90, 103,
  104, 108, 123, 124, 125,
  133, 134, 136, 147,
  148, 163, 164, 167, 185,
  186, 188, 190, 197,
  198, 200, 207, 208, 212
Record Data, 16, 28, 60,
  74, 98, 132, 144, 174, 196
**recording
  observations**, 34–35
**redesign, in design
  process**, 55
repel, 161, 167, 173–174,
  R7
robotics engineer, 48
roots, 185, 188, 189,
  198, 199, R7
ruler, 9

S

safety
  with electronics,
  232–233
  emergency alerts, 138,
  147–151
  in the sun, 106

science tools, 8–9, R8
scientific inquiry, 17–23.
  See also **Inquiry Skills**
  classifying and
  communicating, 20
  comparing, 18
  drawing conclusions,
  33
  hypothesizing and
  planning, 21, 31
  inferring and drawing
  conclusions, 22
  making a model and
  sequence, 23
  observing, 18, 30
  predicting and
  measuring, 19
  recording
  observations, 34–35
  testing, 32
scientists, 1–2
  meteorologists, 101
  thinking like, 30–35
season(s), 103–111, R8
  fall, 108–109
  spring, 104–105
  summer, 106–107
  winter, 81–82, 110–111
seed(s), 201, R8
senses, 3–7, R8
  body parts and, 4–5
  learning with, 6–7
  using, 15–16
sequence, 23, 68–69
Set a Purpose, 15, 27,
  59, 73, 97, 131, 143,
  173, 195

Index

shadows, 131–132
shape, 7
shelter, R9
  for animals, 210–211,
    212, 221
  for beavers, 210
  for clownfish, 207, 210
  for people, 221
  for pets, 214
  for prairie dogs, 210
sight, 7
sirens, 121–122, 148, 149
size, 7
skin, 5
sleet, 90
smell, 7
smoke detector, 138
snow, 89
snowflakes, 89
softness, 136–137
soil, 188, R9
  nutrients from, 198
  for plants, 187, 188,
    198
solids
  rain, 88
  snow, 89
sorting materials, 73–74
sound, 121–122,
  133–139, R9
  emergency alerts, 138,
    147–151
  hearing, 6
  information from,
    138–139
  loudness and softness,
    136–137

  making, 143–144
  pitch, 137
  using, 147–151
  from vibration, 135,
    155–156
space
  for animals, 212
  for pets, 214
  for plants, 189, 190
S pole, 165, 166, 167
spring season,
  104–105
stadium lights, 123
State Your Hypothesis,
  173
steel, magnets and,
  163, 164, 166
S.T.E.M. (Science,
  Technology,
  Engineering, and
  Mathematics).
  See also **Engineering
  and Technology**
  Call Me!, 145–146
  Magnets All Around,
    177–178
  Tool Time, 221–222
  Weather Wisdom:
    Weather Tools,
    115–116
stem(s), 189, 199, 202,
  R10
street lights, 126
summer, 106–107
sunlight, 124, R10
  for plants, 186, 187,
    190, 200

tape measure, 9
taste, 7
technology
  coding, 227–231
  computers, 227–231,
    234
  design process, 49–55
  how engineers work,
    45–55
  magnets, 177–178
  telephones, 145–146
  tools, 221–222
telephones, 145–146
temperature, 86, R10
testing, 32, 54
texture, 6
thermometer, 9, 86, 115
Think About the
  Procedure, 15, 27, 59,
  73, 97, 131, 143, 173,
  195
thunderstorms, 91
tools, 92, 221–222
  for building, 221–222
  measuring, 9
  science, 8–9, R8
  weather, 92–93,
    115–116
tornado, 149, R11
touch, 6
train, maglev, 175–176
train sets, 169
trees
  in fall, 109

© Houghton Mifflin Harcourt Publishing Company

natural materials from, 66

roots, 197

seasonal changes and, 105, 106, 109, 110, 111

in spring, 105

in summer, 107

trunks, 199

in winter, 103, 110, 111

Tssui, Eugene, 75–76

21st Century Skills: Technology and Coding, 227–231

vibrate, 135, R11

water

for animals, 208

ice, 81, 82

for pets, 214

for plants, 186, 187, 190, 200

weather, 81–82, 83–93, R11

measuring, 86–87

observing, 92–93, 97–99

precipitation, 88–91

predicting, 92–93

seasonal patterns of change, 103–111

tools for measuring and tracking, 115–116

tracking, 92–93

types of, 84–85

wind, 84

winter, 81–82

weather alerts, 149

weather balloon, 93

weather pattern(s), 104, R12

fall, 108

spring, 105

summer, 106

winter, 110

weather plane, 115

weather report, 92

weather satellite, 92, 115

weather station, 93

weather tools, 92–93, 115–116

weather vane, 115

weather words, 102

Why It Matters, 10–11, 68–69, 92–93, 126–127, 138–139, 150–151, 168–169, 202–203, 214–215

wind, 84, R12

windshield wipers, 39–40

wind vane, 115

winter, 81–82, 103, 110–111

wood, 61, 64, 65, 66, 67

xylophone, 137

zoo keeper, 219–220